From Phnom Penh
to
Paradise

From Phnom Penh
to
Paradise

Escape from Cambodia

Var Hong Ashe

HODDER AND STOUGHTON
LONDON SYDNEY AUCKLAND TORONTO

TO

SOMALY and PANITA

British Library Cataloguing in Publication Data

Ashe, Var Hong
  From Phnom Penh to paradise: escape from Cambodia.—
  (Hodder Christian paperbacks).
  1. Cambodia—Description and travel— 1975-
  2. Refugees—Cambodia
  3. Escapes—Cambodia
  I. Title
  959.6'04   DS554.382

  ISBN 0-340-41590-8

Contents

Foreword

Kampuchea, and its history, are not well known to the British public. Even if you give it its old name of Cambodia, most people will remember it only from travelogues and as the site of the vast and ancient temple complex of Angkor Wat. This is odd because it has been the scene, since first the French and then the Americans withdrew from South East Asia, of prolonged and increasingly ferocious struggles between contenders for political control of its people.

Perhaps this is because Cambodia's independence was secured in 1954 not from Britain but from France, so not many British people were involved in the country's problems even then. For the next 16 years, it is true, the struggle was between a western form of capitalism and communist revolutionaries. These causes were in confrontation worldwide and it was easy for us to identify – and identify with – them.

But from the fall of Prince Sihanouk in 1970 all the protagonists were communist, none of them had any British connections and, quite simply, many of us lost interest. Yet the scale of the events was so tremendous, and their detail so horrific, that it is surprising we took so little account of them.

My own concern was only awakened when, in 1977, I happened to hear some Thais in Singapore discussing what was going on over their Eastern border under the atrocious government of Pol Pot. As a result I found myself a few days later at Aranya Prathet in Thailand visiting a refugee camp on the Thai–Kampuchean border. After talks with the UN High Commission for Refugees and the Thai Government, I had come as close as I could to the results of the appalling conflict going on within Kampuchea to see them for myself.

7,000 people driven from their homes and often separated from their families by an utterly ruthless political system were housed there in temporary accommodation designed for 4,000. All the facilities were overloaded; the water supply was diminishing; the latrines unspeakable. More refugees were arriving in their hundreds at that and other camps up and down the border. The total number of refugees of all nationalities registered with the United Nations High Commission for Refugees (UNHCR) in camps in Thailand was over 95,000. It was to grow to 270,000 at its peak. (Altogether 653,555 arrived in Thailand between 1977 and early 1986 and 50,141 children were born to them in the camps during that time.)

Nobody was confident that the resettlement programme, headed by UNHCR, could ever catch up with a problem that was getting so far ahead of them, or be sure that the Thais would continue to provide room or resources for so many foreign nationals on their soil. It was costing them a great deal in political terms already.

Under those circumstances one might expect the atmosphere in the camp to be one of sullen apprehension. It was not. Instead I found at its centre a band of dedicated young western volunteers. They came from various countries, but those who particularly caught my attention were a small group of young people sent from Britain by Christian Outreach. They had organised supplemental feeding for all families with children, regular health visits, and a programme of education and retraining for adults as well as children; they had built a special and loving relationship with the refugees; their work was beyond praise. Their leader was Robert Ashe.

Neither he nor I then knew it, but across the border Var Hong, the author of this book, was half-way through the terrifying and painful journey which eventually brought her and her children to that same camp.

This book is the story of that journey, and of its result; it is the story of the triumph of Christian hope in desperate adversity; and it is, beyond expectation, a story with a happy ending. It is worth reading simply for that. But it is also an important document, a record of the hideous extremes of savagery to which political ideologues can take their campaigns – even against their own people – when they believe the ultimate lie: that political reality is the only truth.

This can happen in the West as well as the East. Var Hong's message is a message, therefore, for all of us.

THE LORD ELTON

Acknowledgements

This book principally covers only one part of my life. The years of the Khmer Rouge control of Cambodia were traumatic and many people did not survive. I am alive today only through the grace of God and my first thanks are to Him.

My survival and my very sanity would also have been impossible without my two daughters, Somaly and Panita. They not only reinforced in me a purpose for living, but they took care of me when I was sick. Somaly went out into the forest to search for food. She endured the mosquitoes and insects to find edible vegetation, cooked it and then fed me. Panita was too young and often too sick to accompany her, but her innocent eyes and smiling face gave me much encouragement in the struggle for survival. This book is dedicated to them to emphasise my love for them and to show them my appreciation for their support during those years.

Many people have helped me practically and given me emotional support over the years: Pat and Marion Ashe, who lovingly welcomed me to England and into their family; Patsy and Reggie Merryweather, who 'adopted' me as if I was their own daughter; Katherine Rowen-Robinson and Helen and Derek Taylor Thompson, who caringly helped with Somaly's and Panita's education; Suzie and Jonathan Wood, who have been wonderful guardians for my daughters while I have been away from England; all those in Godalming, my first home in England – Rae and Harvey Williams, Claire and Lionel East, Laura and John

Acknowledgements

Clarke, Sheila and Brian Ward, Monica Lucey, Olwen and George Hayes, David Bookham, Elizabeth Jenkins and many, many more – to whom the fact that I was a refugee was immaterial. They treated me as a human being in need of help and I will be forever grateful to them.

In Thailand, I have omitted the names of many who helped me, since the mention of their names would not be helpful to them in the continuance of their work in the politically complex task of assisting refugees. None the less, their names are recorded in my mind and I will not forget their kindness. I can mention the names of Julian Manyon and David Mills, from the *TV Eye* programme of Thames Television, who were instrumental in highlighting the problems of the Cambodian refugees and in expediting my application for an entry visa to Britain. My thanks go to Dr John Napponnick, who treated me when I was sick in Thailand, and to Dr Michel Gabaudan who, assisted by John, carried out a skin graft on my hand.

I am also indebted to Homer Dowdy, who edited this story with understanding and wisdom, and who, together with his wife Nancy, lovingly encouraged me in getting it finished.

My thanks are incomplete without mentioning my mother, whose love for me extended through her blindness, and without whose physical support for my daughters and for me life would have been extremely difficult.

And last, but not least, my thanks go to my husband, Robert, who has given me a new life in England and who supported and helped me in the writing of this book.

Front cover inset photo: Var, Panita and Somaly at the Aranya Prathet refugee camp. (Photo: TV Eye).

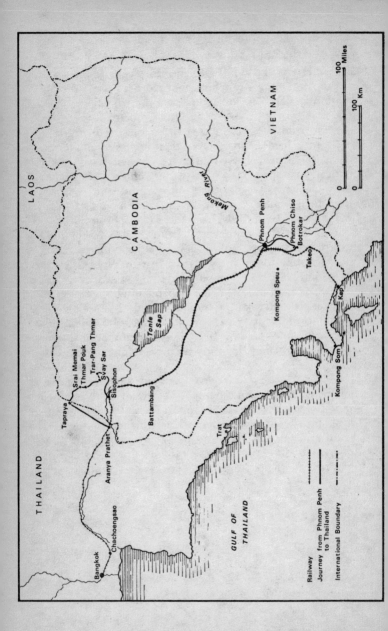

Preface

Cambodia – for a long time the word brought to mind a gentle and beautiful nation in South-East Asia where most of the people were engaged in a peaceful existence cultivating rice in the countryside. It is claimed that the original Khmer[1] kingdom was founded in the 1st century AD and was called Fu-nan. This was defeated in war around the 6th century by the neighbouring kingdom of Chen-la. Following more fighting in the late 7th century, a new king assumed the throne in 802 and this marked the beginning of the Kampuchea or Angkor[2] period of Cambodia. During the next 500 years, Cambodia reached its peak in culture and in the acquisition of territory. Some of present-day Thailand, Laos, and Vietnam used to be part of a great Khmer empire. However, Cambodia declined due to internal peasant revolts and external attacks from neighbouring countries. In 1431, the then Cambodian capital, Angkor Thom, was captured by the Thais and, although the Khmers recaptured it eventually, this marked the end of the great Angkor period.

For the next four centuries, Cambodia struggled to survive as Thailand and Vietnam jostled for control. Little by little both Vietnam and Thailand began to annex parts of the old Khmer Empire. Only internal dissension and civil

---

[1] 'Khmer' is an alternative word for 'Cambodian'.
[2] 'Kampuchea' is the original name for Cambodia. Angkor was the name of the ancient capital of Cambodia.

war in Vietnam and external attacks on Thailand from Burma prevented the complete partition of Cambodia.

Finally, in 1864, Cambodia signed a treaty with France which established Cambodia as a French protectorate and later as a French colony. Cambodia was virtually ruled by France for the next 90 years, only interrupted briefly by the Japanese occupation during the Second World War. Prince Norodom Sihanouk was selected as king in 1941 and managed to bring Cambodia to full independence by 1954. In 1955 he abdicated the throne in favour of his father, and entered into the political arena. He became Prime Minister and later Head of State. Throughout the 1960s, Sihanouk walked a tightrope of neutrality, trying to stay out of the war which was engulfing Vietnam and Laos. He was reasonably successful, although both rightist and leftist elements took to the jungles to oppose him. The leftist opponents were called the Khmer Rouge (Red Khmers) and were led by French-educated dissidents under Pol Pot, Ieng Sary and Khieu Samphan.

In early 1970, Prince Sihanouk was deposed and the monarchy abolished. A Khmer republic was established under the leadership of General Lon Nol, who was then supported by the United States. Sihanouk went to Peking, where he allied himself with the Khmer Rouge to try and regain control of his country. He was made titular Head of State for the Khmer Rouge government-in-exile, but actual control of the Khmer Rouge movement and army remained firmly in the hands of the communists. Between 1970 and 1975, civil war raged throughout Cambodia. A brief incursion by the South Vietnamese Army and US troops in the border areas was followed by heavy US bombing raids on suspected Khmer Rouge and North Vietnamese positions inside Cambodia. Many of the bombs fell on innocent villages and ruined vast tracts of agricultural land. Non-communist peasants, driven from their homes by the bombing and fed up with the corruption that prevailed in the Lon Nol government, either volunteered for or were coerced into joining the Khmer Rouge army. Emotions ran high on both sides of the fighting and horrific acts of brutality were reported. In general, the Khmer Rouge came to be feared and were thought to show no mercy when fighting.

By early 1975, Cambodia had almost beaten itself to death. Millions of people had been displaced by the fighting and both agricultural and industrial production was almost at a standstill. The majority of the population were sickened and exhausted by the continual violence and wanted only to see an end to the bloodshed. None of us could foresee that the blood-letting was only just beginning and that the Khmer Rouge would embark on a four-year reign of terror which has rarely been equalled in the world. My family and I became the victims of the new society which the Khmer Rouge had imposed upon Cambodia. Throughout the destruction of our country's culture, religion and government, and of social and family ties, some of us survived. Many did not.

To assist the reader to better understand the relationship between the people in this book, the following list and description is given:

Somaly	— my older daughter
Panita	— my younger daughter
An, Rathana and Peauv	— my three younger brothers
Sokhon, Da and Srey Vy	— my three younger sisters
Aheng	— Panita's nanny
Lay	— Sokhon's fiancé
Hear	— Lay's older brother
Lach Virak Phong	— my first husband
Taing Chhaya	— my mother
Hong Yang	— my father

1 The Fall of Phnom Penh

As I walked reluctantly down the stairs, a terrible fear gripped my heart. I was too frightened to go, but duty drove me on. Still indecisive, I found myself standing next to my car. Opening the door, I breathed a prayer: "Lord, please use the roof of my car to shield me from the rockets."

It seemed only moments later when I could hear explosions all around me as I weaved in and out of the traffic in my Opel Rekord. It was April 14th, 1975, and the communist noose around Phnom Penh, the capital of Cambodia, was tightening remorselessly. Each day, the government troops under our corrupt dictator, Lon Nol, were slowly retreating towards the centre of the capital. Three million Cambodians, mostly refugees from the ravaged provinces in the countryside, huddled in an ever-decreasing area hoping in vain for a miracle which would save us from devastation.

In what must have seemed like an act of utter folly, I was now driving against the flow of traffic which was fleeing into the inner sanctuary of Phnom Penh. Mine was almost the only vehicle driving out of the city towards the heaviest area of bombardment around the suburb of Toul Kauk. Only the day before, I had driven in the opposite direction carrying the members of my family to safety. One of my younger brothers, Rathana, had refused to come with us. His main purpose in life was to study, and he had been unwilling to exchange our relatively spacious home for the cramped conditions of our temporary refuge in the city centre. Without him, and fearful for his safety, my mother had spent the night in tears and had begged me to return and fetch him. I was the only member of the family present who could drive and there was no one else who could go. Almost too afraid to agree to her request, it was none the less my duty, and I had left against my better judgement.

Now, as the rockets seemed to be falling like rain, I prayed constantly, asking God to protect me. Several times my fear nearly compelled me to turn back, but the thought of failing my mother spurred me on. I passed many casualties of the exploding rockets. Parents were running with wounded children in their arms, their shirts bright red with blood. Little three-wheeled taxis, their floors awash with blood, bore the wounded away to already overcrowded hospitals. There was chaos everywhere and a sense of panic gripped the population.

Phnom Penh had once been a beautiful city of about half a million, with tree-lined boulevards and friendly crowds. Now, buildings were shattered by the shelling, the population had swollen to three million with displaced people fleeing in from the countryside, and the streets were littered with rubbish and the flotsam and jetsam of war.

I finally reached the area of Toul Kauk, where it seemed that hardly any life remained. Those who had not been killed by rockets had either fled in terror or had imprisoned themselves in underground bunkers with a stock of food. With smoke billowing from the burning houses, it had become like a ghost town. It was a complete contrast to the rushing crowds which I had passed earlier, and I was able to speed down unobstructed roads towards our home.

I skidded to a halt in front of our gate, which was tightly closed.

"Rathana, Rathana," I screamed desperately between the mounting crescendo of explosions. I caught sight of my brother's face peering out of our underground bunker, and he came running towards the gate to check that it was really me.

"Come quickly – we must return at once to the city centre," I ordered breathlessly.

"No," he replied. "I'm not going to that small room with so many people. How can I possibly study? I want to stay here."

Shocked, I could hardly believe what I was hearing. Almost angrily, I began to argue with him.

"I've risked my life to come and get you. You must come – Mother is very worried about you."

To any outside observer, we must have looked completely crazy, standing there having an argument over the gate while rockets exploded all around us. Eventually Rathana agreed to come with me and I breathed a sigh of relief. However, even in my fear and hurry to get away, I was still thinking of the hard floor which awaited me at our new home in the city. My car was still full of clothes and a few valuable items which I had packed in on my first trip into the city. I had not bothered to unload them because I felt we would only be away for a short time. I had taken them in case our house was either rocketed or looted during our absence. Now, I rushed inside the house and grabbed my mattress. Dragging it outside, Rathana and I slung it on the car roof and quickly tied it down. The only thing that Rathana took was a bag of books. "I can live in one set of clothes," he explained, "but I can't live without my books."

I put the car into gear and, with a screech of tyres, we left. As we drove out of Toul Kauk, we passed a Land-Rover. Looking across, I saw that it was Kong Suosdey, the daughter of General Kong Chhath. We were good friends and she yelled through the open window, "What on earth are you doing with that mattress?" She could not imagine that anyone in their right mind would want to drive into such an inferno of destruction simply to rescue a mattress.

She laughed, waved and drove quickly away. I have never seen her since.

We joined the long queue of traffic back into Phnom Penh and arrived at the four-storey shophouse which was to be our home for the next few days. On the ground floor was a tyre shop which belonged to Hear. His brother, Lay, was engaged to my younger sister, Sokhon, and his family had kindly offered us shelter during those troubled times.

On the third floor, which consisted of a single room running the whole 13-metre length of the building, were crowded 16 people, including Lay's family. Our family was not quite complete. My mother was there, but my father, who was a colonel in the Cambodian army, was away. He had been sent almost a month earlier to take charge of a battalion of troops guarding the approaches to west Phnom Penh. Since then, our only contact with him had been in the form of messages carried by his chauffeur. Apart from him, two others were missing.

My husband, Lach Virak Phong, whose comfort and support I needed desperately, was 8,000 miles away. He had left Phnom Penh in August 1974 to take up a scholarship and to complete his studies at the International Institute of Educational Planning in Paris. The war had seemed far away from Phnom Penh at that time and he had gone without knowing that events would soon overtake us all. None of us had realised that government troops would crumble so rapidly before the final onslaught of the Khmer Rouge.

The other person missing was my younger brother, An, who was a second lieutenant in the army. Like my father, he too was away fighting at the front.

My two daughters, Somaly, aged six years, and Panita, only 18 months, were with me in Phnom Penh. I came back into the room to find Aheng, Panita's nanny, playing with them both. My other brother, Peauv, and sisters, Sokhon, Da and Srey Vy, came forward to welcome us

back from Toul Kauk. All of my brothers and sisters —
except for Sokhon who was old enough to work — would
normally have been at school in more peaceful times instead
of hiding from rockets fired by our own people.

The rest of the day and night passed uneventfully, but
in the morning Rathana announced that he was returning
to our home in Toul Kauk. Throughout the night he
had listened to the distant sound of explosions gradually
decrease in intensity. He calmly announced that, since the
danger was now past, he intended to return home where
there was sufficient space and peace to study. We stared at
him incredulously. My mother pleaded with him to stay,
but to no avail. He was stubborn and wanted only to be
left to his studies. As he walked out through the door,
clutching his precious bag of books, my mother was speechless. We watched through the window as Rathana walked
away from us down the street. Not knowing how quickly
Phnom Penh would fall to the Khmer Rouge, Rathana was
separated from us and disappeared.

That afternoon and evening we talked quietly among
ourselves, wondering whether the government troops
would be able to beat back the Khmer Rouge attack. They
had attacked before and failed. Surely they would fail again.
The relative calm compared to the earlier shelling led us to
believe that it might soon be safe for us to return to our
homes.

Renewed fighting in the night, and the sudden arrival of
An the next morning, shattered our hopes. In the early
hours of the morning An had left his army unit at Kompong
Speu, a province about 40 miles west of Phnom Penh,
when it had been overrun by the Khmer Rouge. Like many
other soldiers fleeing in front of the rapidly advancing
enemy, he had thrown away his uniform and had disguised
himself as a civilian. Having made his way to join us, he
went in and out of the house continuously in an effort to
find out what was going on. He told us of the rapid

advances being made by the Khmer Rouge troops and of the crumbling resistance of the government forces. He felt it would not be long before the Khmer Rouge entered the main part of the city.

We waited. It was hot and stuffy in our single room but, apart from An, no one dared to go out. The night passed slowly and we awoke to a memorable morning. The date, April 17th, 1975, would stay in the minds of millions for years to come. It marked the beginning of almost four years of terror as the Khmer Rouge turned Cambodia into a vast concentration camp.

The telephone rang, making us all jump. We were in a nervous mood as we could hear the sound of machine-gun fire coming closer and closer. My mother picked up the telephone and, almost unbelievably, heard my father's voice. As he spoke, we clustered round the telephone with growing excitement. He was still alive and we yearned desperately for him to be with us. My mother pleaded with him to make his way to the house or to hide from the conquering Khmer Rouge. When he said that he could not leave his troops, she tried to persuade him to disguise himself as an ordinary soldier. My father was adamant that he would neither hide nor run away. He tried to console us by saying that he was well known and respected for his honesty. He was sure that the Khmer Rouge would need people like himself to help rebuild the country after the devastation of the war. As my mother said a tearful good-bye, a feeling of helplessness settled over us. We had all been very close to our father and had loved him for his gentleness. I was 26 years of age and the oldest of the children. Without him, I felt the heavy responsibility for our family. We hungered for the strength and leadership which our father had always given to us. This was our last contact with him and we were never to see him again.

Around midday we heard shouts and screams of delight amidst the roar of tanks and other heavy vehicles. From our high vantage point, we could see the continuous advance of small groups of Khmer Rouge down the street and the almost rapturous welcome demonstrated by the citizens of Phnom Penh. Their enthusiasm was infectious and we joined with many others to wave white flags from our windows and to cheer the black-clad communist soldiers. Some of us, witnessing this spontaneous outburst of joy, dared to hope that the Khmer Rouge victory would bring peace to our troubled land. For too long, Khmer had been pitted against Khmer and the once beautiful countryside of Cambodia had been destroyed by the savagery of war. In the countryside, peasants had lived in terror as waves of American B52 bombers had dropped their inhuman cargoes to tear apart the peaceful rice paddies. Was it now possible, we asked ourselves, that we could at last live in peace, even though our new rulers would be communists? As these jungle fighters passed down the streets, their firm blank looks and silent faces seemed an ominous portent of events to come.

Shortly before 1 p.m. the martial music, which had been playing almost continuously on the radio, was interrupted by an announcement. The speaker was General Mey Si-chan, one of the government leaders, and he spoke of negotiations which were in progress with the Khmer Rouge. As he was speaking, his announcement was abruptly broken off and a new voice cut in angrily to say that there were no negotiations, only complete victory by the Khmer Rouge. After a long silence, another Khmer Rouge leader announced that all government officials were to report immediately to the Ministry of Information. He went on to say that the Khmer Rouge victory was complete and that the officials of the old regime were needed to help organise and rebuild the country. He ended by praising the People's National Liberation Front of Kampuchea, which had made possible the victory of the glorious revolution.

We sat stunned in front of the radio and our earlier

feelings of joy quickly dissipated with the realisation that things were not going well. In the afternoon, An returned from one of his forays to say that he had seen the Khmer Rouge ransacking many of the pharmacies and food stores. The medicines and food were loaded on to trucks which were driven off along roads which led out of the city. An sensed that the war was not yet over and that worse was to come. A feeling of gloom settled over us.

The rest of the afternoon passed slowly. We tried to while away the time by talking or playing cards but, for the most part, we simply sat and waited. Since nearly all the shooting had ceased, we decided that we would stay one more night and then make our way back to our own home in Toul Kauk.

That night we huddled together for comfort, but sleep was slow to come. The day had been filled with emotion and the thought of our uncertain future lay heavily over us. I lay close to my daughters, Somaly and Panita. I felt overwhelmed with guilt because Virak Phong had begged me several times in his letters to leave Cambodia with our children and to join him in Paris. I had kept putting off the departure, thinking that it would be a waste of money and never really believing that Phnom Penh would fall to the communists, until it was too late. As the Khmer Rouge neared Phnom Penh, their rockets had turned the runways of Pochentong Airport into rubble, making it impossible for us to leave. Although I was surrounded by my mother and other brothers and sisters, I felt truly alone. In my desperation and in the quiet darkness, broken now occasionally by distant bursts of gunfire, I prayed to the God whom I had asked to take over my life only four months earlier. I had much to learn about God and about how to pray, but I knew that He cared for me and loved me. As I prayed now, a sense of calm stole over me and I felt the reassurance, which would often come to me in the years ahead, that God was powerful enough to care for us all.

April 18 dawned and we began to wake up around 7 a.m. Looking out of the windows, we could see many people moving in different directions. We were about to pack our belongings and leave for home when An returned from another of his fact-finding trips.

"Everyone is leaving the city. The Khmer Rouge are forcing everyone out of their houses. There's absolute chaos in the streets," he announced breathlessly. His description of events caused panic in the house. "They have told everyone this so that they can clear out the remaining elements of the US-backed Lon Nol forces whom they claim are still resisting. I've been to different parts of the city and I overheard some people being told to go only for three hours, while others were told to leave for one to three days."

An rattled off more details of what he had seen and my mind contemplated the future. What fate awaited us outside Phnom Penh? My family were all city people and the thought of having to survive in the countryside filled me with apprehension.

I turned to An and asked him, "What do you think we should do? With so many people in the streets, it will be dangerous and difficult to keep together." The others joined in. "It's safe here for now and we have a little food. Let's wait and see." I looked over at my mother and she nodded slowly in agreement. None of us wanted to go and An counselled us to wait in the shophouse for further developments.

A little later on, a loudspeaker truck moved slowly down the street, ordering everyone to leave the city or face the consequences of getting hurt. We were afraid to stay, but we were more afraid to go. We quietly drew the curtains and waited, trying not to make any noise. Our little store of food would last for several days and the water supply was still functioning.

In the early evening we could see Khmer Rouge vehicles

in the streets below looting the shops. Most of the inhabitants had already fled, leaving the doors securely bolted. When the young communists, who were from simple backgrounds, were unable to break open the doors, they stood back and fired a B40 rocket which completely destroyed the doors and much of the shop's contents. Opposite our hideout was a shop stocked full of canned and preserved foods. It had a solid door and the B40 rocket which the Khmer Rouge fired succeeded only in buckling the metal. Undaunted, they hitched a GMC truck to the doors with a length of chain and ripped them from their hinges. Mercifully, the tyre shop beneath us was of no interest to the Khmer Rouge and they passed us by.

By keeping quiet we were able to stay hidden for four days. Peering through the curtains each day, we watched the long lines of people pass by on their way out of the city. Gradually the lines thinned out and the numbers dwindled. On the morning of the 21st, the streets around us were almost deserted except for a group of Khmer Rouge armed with AK47 automatic rifles and B40 rocket launchers. They were going into all the houses to check for occupants. Coming to the tyre shop below us, they rattled the locked doors and shouted, "Hey, anyone inside? Come on out immediately or there will be severe punishment." My heart was pounding as I tried desperately to keep Panita from making any sound. They rattled the doors some more and then we heard subdued conversation as they discussed among themselves. Apparently satisfied that there was no one inside, the Khmer Rouge went on down the street. We all heaved a sigh of relief and started breathing again.

However, our relief was short-lived. Two hours later, we heard sounds coming from the roof top. The Khmer Rouge soldiers had crept over the roof from another house and entered through a door on the fourth floor above us. We crouched in terror, expecting a hail of bullets, and I clutched Panita and Somaly to me in an effort to shield them. Suddenly, five young Khmer Rouge bounded through the doorway with their rifles pointed straight at us. The blood drained from my face and I went cold with terror. Silently, they stared at us. Then their leader, seeing my mother and Lay's mother, smiled, relaxing the tension in an instant. He turned to them out of respect for older people.

"Mother,"[1] he said, "we won't harm you. Please leave the city for three days. Take food for your children, but you must leave immediately. We are here because we care for your lives. We know it's difficult for you to live outside the city, but you'll be happier after we've arranged everything. We have fought for five years, not caring for our lives, just to help you and to relieve your suffering under the corrupt Lon Nol government supported by the American imperialists."

His smile and this short speech made us feel that everything would be all right. Everyone started to speak at once, shouting questions, clamouring for answers. Where would we live? How would we travel? What would we eat? At this, the Khmer Rouge leader shouted angrily: "Now, if you don't want to listen, don't say that we have no compassion. We will give you an hour to leave and it is up to you to decide. However, you must be responsible for your own actions."

Our fear returned greater than before, and we agreed to leave immediately. The sight of their rifles pointed straight at our hearts left us in no doubt as to the consequences for disobedience to these Khmer Rouge.

We quickly made ready for our departure. Clothes were thrown aside in favour of food, as we had no idea what we would find outside the city. While we could live without a second set of clothes, we would die without food. For

---

[1] The Khmer Rouge always called older people 'Father' and 'Mother', while all other ages were addressed as 'Mit', which is a Khmer word meaning 'Comrade'.

myself, I filled a large one-gallon kettle with rice and struggled downstairs with my two children and the rest of the two families. I didn't think about how we were going to cook the rice and completely forgot about cooking pots and matches, although fortunately some of the others remembered. In the road outside the shop, we found that my car was still intact. Lay's eldest brother, Hear, owned a brand-new jeep which he didn't want to take. He was afraid that the Khmer Rouge might confiscate it and he preferred to leave it in the shop in the hope that it would still be there when he returned. Throwing all the food packs into my car, I climbed in to steer. Due to the hierarchy within the social classes which still existed, my mother was considered to be the most senior and she was allowed to sit in the passenger seat. Everyone else, except little Panita, either pushed the car or walked alongside. The weight of all the food in the car proved to be almost too much, because it was still loaded down with the clothes and other valuables which I had not had time to unpack.

After some discussion, we decided to take the jeep as well and the load was evenly distributed between the two vehicles. Each of the two cars had petrol in its tank, but we were afraid to start the engines in case the Khmer Rouge confiscated the cars. While An had been moving around the city during his trips out of the house, he had seen many cars confiscated by the Khmer Rouge. Some of the young soldiers, who had been fighting for years in the jungle, were totally ignorant about vehicles, but they became excited like little children with a new toy whenever they had the chance to drive off in a car. Another of our reasons for not starting up the engines was to save the petrol in case we needed it in an emergency later on. We saw no chance of being able to replenish our petrol supply along the way.

With everyone lending a hand to push, our two-car convoy set off into the unknown.

2   Flight from Phnom Penh

Our sad little convoy moved slowly along the streets. It was hard work for those pushing and people took it in turns except for the young children and the very old. Initially, Khmer Rouge soldiers ordered us to go to the east. We obeyed their instructions although we were reluctant to do so, having no connections with the eastern parts of Cambodia. My mother felt that Takeo, in the south, was the most sensible place to aim for. All of our family had been born there and she felt that others who were missing might try and reach there as well.

As in most Khmer families, my mother was the most influential when it came to making family decisions. Although there might be some discussion about it, she would always have the final word and the rest of us would fall into line. Now, we accepted her decision that we should head for Takeo and we looked for an opportunity to change direction.

At the beginning of our trek, the streets were almost deserted, and it seemed that we were some of the last people to leave the city centre. However, we soon came across small groups of people who were also in the process of hurriedly leaving the city under the threats from the Khmer Rouge. Obviously the Khmer Rouge were clearing out one section of the city at a time. As we pressed forward and the numbers of people increased, it proved to be impossible to move faster than at a walking pace. To lessen the possibility of confiscation, Hear stopped his jeep at the nearest puddle and, with the help of his brothers, daubed mud mixed with old engine oil all over it. Being brand new, it was an obvious attraction to the Khmer Rouge, who were eager to pick up any useful transport, especially jeeps and Land-Rovers.

Along each side of the road in the commercial districts, broken shop doors swung open to reveal their looted interiors. The most popular shops appeared to be those containing food, cloth or pharmaceutical supplies. Many stores selling luxury goods, such as electrical items and cosmetics, had been emptied but their contents were left scattered on the roadside.

A general air of misery hung over the whole crowd as we trudged along. Our entire fabric of life had been torn apart and, as I stared at a sea of unknown faces, my own uncertainty was mirrored in the looks which I received back. I had never seen the streets so packed with people before. Some, like us, were pushing cars; others pushed carts or bicycles with packages piled high behind the seat, so heavy that it seemed as if only the denseness of the crowd prevented them from falling over. Others, who were poorer, and those who had been evacuated with little or no warning, carried bags on their heads or on the ends of bamboo poles slung over their shoulders. Some walked only with a bunch of house keys in their hands, hoping to go back before too long. When their hunger became acute and they realised the danger of starving, some were clever enough to search the empty houses along the road for food.

By midday, the ever watchful Khmer Rouge seemed to have disappeared. Perhaps they had simply gone off to have lunch, but we seized our opportunity and turned off the main road into a street leading south. The number of people thronging the street seemed smaller and we hurried along as fast as we could, spurred on by the sound of machine-gun fire which drifted to our ears from behind. Within half-an-hour we came across another Khmer Rouge patrol who ordered us to turn into a road going west. The evacuation of the city seemed a very haphazard affair with little coordination between the different groups of Khmer Rouge cadres.

As we pushed westwards, we occasionally passed the bodies of government soldiers which had been left lying on the side of the road where they had been shot. The tropical heat had caused rapid decomposition and the skin was blackened under the sun. A cloud of flies swarmed around each body and already the maggots were at work eating the putrid flesh. It was an awful sight and I could only wonder at the agony of those who had lost husbands, fathers and brothers in this way.

The crowds in the road had thickened again, but they parted to allow through a Khmer Rouge jeep making a loudspeaker announcement. Anyone holding a rifle or pistol was ordered to hand them over immediately or face a charge of being a counter-revolutionary. An iron hand seemed to tighten around my heart. I was suddenly afraid as I remembered that, hidden in the boot of my car, were two M16 automatic rifles, two revolvers and an air-rifle. I had brought them from my house in Toul Kauk when we had moved to the city centre, and I had left them packed in the boot. In our hurry to leave that morning, I had completely forgotten about them and they lay still hidden in my car. During the chaotic days prior to the fall of the city, it had seemed sensible to have some form of protection. Now the very thing that we had thought would give us security might mean our death.

We debated what to do and had just come to a decision to hand them over, when we observed another man surrender his weapon to a Khmer Rouge soldier. He was immediately detained for questioning and not allowed to continue on his journey. Perhaps the Khmer Rouge reasoned that he should have surrendered it several days before and suspected him of being against the new regime. Since we were in a similar situation, our fear redoubled; so we carried on, hoping for a chance to dump the weapons later on.

In the early afternoon we passed a large villa by the side of the road. The children were becoming very hungry, so we stopped to cook rice which we ate together with some canned food. Since I had a fairly easy job in steering the car, instead of pushing it like the others, I had taken it upon myself to cook for the whole group. It was a difficult learning process for me as I had hardly ever done any cooking before. There had always been a cook in my house since my childhood, and it now seemed an almost impossible task to cook for all the 27 people in our group. I am sure that hunger as well as the uncertainty of the whole situation enabled people to ignore the none-too-exciting taste of my initial attempts at cooking. While the others were eating, An and I went out to the car to try to get rid of the weapons. As An packed them into an old canvas kitbag, together with some clothes to disguise the shape, I pretended to shield him from the sun with an old piece of cloth so that no one would see the weapons. In this way we were able to take the guns into a villa and abandon them in a cupboard.

On the way back to the car we were spotted by some Khmer Rouge soldiers. Seeing the kitbag in An's hand and recognising it as being of military issue, they became suspicious. "Stop right there and don't move," they yelled. I began to shake with fear as they came running over holding their AK47s in the firing position. "Open the bag," one of them shouted at An. He opened it up slowly and one of the soldiers grabbed it away from him. While the others covered us with their weapons, he went through it by throwing all the clothes on to the ground. Finding no weapons, he stood up and commanded: "All right, you can put everything back. Hurry up and move out of the city. There's no time to waste eating food." With that, they swung around to continue with their patrol. Our narrow escape left us trembling with relief. We wanted to stay in the villa, but the last order from the Khmer Rouge sent us hurrying on our way.

There were four or five major highways leading out of Phnom Penh, but with the original 600,000 residents swollen with refugees from the countryside to an estimated three million people, each highway must have been clogged with its human traffic jam for miles. Certainly our road, already full, was becoming more packed as side-streets disgorged their jostling thousands. Many people wanted to go south-east along the Mekong River. Everyone was worried about water as we were now in the middle of the dry season, and the Mekong could supply not only water but fish as well. However, since we were all leaving several days after the first exodus, too many people had already taken that road and the Khmer Rouge forced us westwards. At times it seemed almost as if we were in the middle of a whirlpool with people going round and round in circles. Those from behind pushed forwards, urged on by the guns of the Khmer Rouge, while those in front dragged their heels, unwilling to go west into a poor part of Cambodia and still hoping for a quick return to the city.

By late afternoon, we arrived at a spot on the outskirts of Phnom Penh where the main highway to the west began. Several other roads fed into the highway at the same place and we saw a mass of people coming from all directions. It was here that I witnessed some of the most terrible scenes which remain imprinted on my mind to this day. Among the crowds were sick and wounded people who had clearly only recently been evacuated from a hospital. Several, still in their hospital beds, were being pushed along by their relatives. One man was in a wheel chair with blood still oozing from the bandages which covered the stumps of his amputated legs. A number of families carried their ageing parents in hammocks slung over their shoulders. Some of the old people could be heard telling their children: "I'm old now, and you'll only exhaust yourselves carrying me. Leave me to die." In contrast to this, an old woman pleaded amidst floods of tears with her children to keep on carrying her and not to leave her to die along the road. We could see the exhausted faces of her children, sick with despair, as they struggled along. On the side of the road, a woman was giving birth to her baby, and relatives scurried to and fro in the crowd searching for a midwife to help.

The heat, the dust, the crying children, the lack of food and water, and the terror combined together to begin a breakdown of social and family structures and ties. For some of the rural peasants, it meant a bonanza as they looted houses alongside the road and sold the food to those who had fled with nothing. There were many people who had believed the Khmer Rouge when told that they would only be away from their homes for a few hours or a day at the most. Such people had left with only a bunch of keys and were now desperate for food. The Khmer Rouge had already announced that money currently in circulation was valueless, but everyone, especially the peasants, refused to believe it. Now, having looted houses along the roadside, they were busy setting up impromptu markets and selling food at five times the already inflated Phnom Penh prices. In this way, some of the poor quickly became paper million-aires, collecting vast amounts of notes which could only be used later on for burning or for making paper bags.

As the massive crowds rushed together, some families became separated and we often passed little children and women weeping by the roadside as they contemplated a future without their loved ones. For our group of 27 people, the two cars served as a landmark so that even when we became separated we could still see the cars in the distance and could force our way back to them. The adults in our party constantly checked to see that the children were still with us, and in this way we arrived in the early evening at a large villa set back from the road. We couldn't get inside the villa because it was already packed with refugees from the city. Instead, we found shelter in the large garden and we settled down to an uneasy sleep.

That night, two old people died inside the large house. One, an old man, simply died of old age. The other, a woman, died from a heart attack. The night air was filled with the sound of weeping as the two families gave vent to their grief. Our family felt the tragedy as well, realising that it might have been our own mother, and cried also in sympathy.

Dawn broke to reveal the crowds still trudging past on the road. We still believed that we might be able to return after only a few days and were, therefore, reluctant to go far out of the city as we would only have a long way to return. Thus for the whole of the second day, we concealed ourselves and waited in the grounds of the villa.

In the early hours of the third day after our departure from the city centre, the Khmer Rouge arrived and told each group in the villa to keep moving along the highway. They didn't say where we should go, but just told us to keep moving. Many people were disappointed and wanted to go back to their homes. Few people left until the Khmer Rouge, becoming angry, began firing their guns into the air. The sound of the automatic rifle fire was deafening and we tensed with shock. Our limbs were like jelly and we trembled like leaves in the wind. Our only thought was to reload the cars and go – to where, we didn't know.

As we left the villa, we decided to take a chance and attempt to go southwards. It meant having to go back towards Phnom Penh for a short distance to reach the turning to the south. It was only thanks to the strength of Lay and his brothers that we were able to push the two cars against the flow of the people. Whenever we saw Khmer Rouge soldiers, we stopped and the men went away from the cars while the women and children pretended to be resting. When the soldiers told us to turn back, we agreed immediately but, as soon as the Khmer Rouge went away, the men rejoined us and we continued pushing. Within half an hour we had reached the side road to the south and quickly mingled with everyone else going along that road.

It wasn't long before we began to feel thirsty, and we stopped while one of Lay's brothers went off to search for water. While he was away, the Khmer Rouge came to order us to keep moving and we were forced to continue our journey without him. Within a mile the Khmer Rouge had disappeared again, and we stopped while Hear sent his brothers back to look for the missing one. While waiting with Hear, we noticed a putrid smell from close at hand. Not far away, we could make out the corpses of two government soldiers. Their bodies were bloated with the heat and the maggots were already crawling over them. It turned our stomachs and made our waiting a real struggle. Fortunately, before long, everyone returned having found the missing brother and we all set off once more.

By midday, we had arrived at the southern edge of the city. We passed one of the largest Phnom Penh hospitals, L'Hôpital Khmero-Soviétique. It was a distressing sight. Many patients were waving from the hospital yard pleading for help, while the walking sick and wounded lined the hospital driveway. Occasionally some people arrived at the hospital and were able to find a sick or wounded relative, whom they immediately escorted from the hospital still lying in their sick-bed. No doctors or nurses were to be seen as the whole medical staff had been driven away by the Khmer Rouge. I watched with a feeling of helplessness as dozens, too tired to drag themselves away, lay there with arms outstretched pleading for help. Physically and emotionally exhausted, responsible for a traumatised mother – who had herself only recently been discharged from a clinic after having both eyes operated on for cataracts – and two daughters and several other younger brothers and sisters, I felt overwhelmed with the enormity of the problem.

Two miles past the hospital, we stopped to cook lunch. It was already mid-afternoon and everyone was exhausted. It wasn't hard to come to the decision to settle down for the night right where we were. Along with so many thousands of others, we clung desperately to the hope that we would eventually be allowed to return to Phnom Penh. It seemed inconceivable that our new rulers would want to leave the capital empty for more than a few days. In the history of the whole world, we had never heard of a revolution which had emptied the capital and which had not allowed the population to return. Why should they keep us away from our homes? Surely they needed the skilled city people to help rebuild the country into a strong independent power? We found it difficult to accept that we were not going back.

That evening the men in our group went off to search for food in the deserted houses along the road. We found ourselves in one of the most exclusive areas of Phnom Penh. Only half a kilometre away lay the plush residence of Lon Nol, President of the Khmer Republic, who had fled from his country only days before the communists swept into Phnom Penh. Other large villas lined the road and Lay's brothers easily found six 50 kg sacks of rice and some useful garden tools which we loaded into the jeep.

Early the following morning, An took me to see a nearby house where he had found a large food supply. The owners must have been very rich and had stored huge stocks of food to see them through a shortage. We found about twenty 100 kg sacks of rice, 30 large jars of preserved meat, many sacks of charcoal and several cans of cooking oil. People kept tramping past us to take out supplies as if they were going into a supermarket, and we also took what we could carry.

Before leaving that morning, we all gathered together to talk about the two cars. It was becoming too tiring to push both of them, and so it was decided to abandon mine. We transferred all the food to the jeep. From my car I took out one small bag of belongings and a bag of medicine for my stomach ulcer from which I had suffered for nearly a year. However, I left behind three large suitcases of clothes, some silverware and other items which I had saved from my home in Phnom Penh. As I abandoned these trappings of my civilised world, I cried – especially when another family immediately behind us grabbed all my things to put on top of their own car.

We left in the jeep. I steered with my mother in the passenger seat and little Panita lying on top of the bags. Somaly walked alongside while the men pushed. Hear carried his own small daughter on his shoulders and Somaly watched them with sadness in her eyes. Later on, she whispered quietly to me, "I wish Papa was here to carry me." Already she was missing her father, who was so many thousands of miles away. Before long we came to a part of the road where the Khmer Rouge were confiscating vehicles. Hear had already removed the spark plugs so that the jeep wouldn't start and, since he had covered it with mud and old oil, it looked quite old. When the Khmer Rouge told him to hand over the jeep, he told them that it wasn't his and that the engine wouldn't work. The Khmer Rouge tried to start the jeep but, being unable to do so, allowed us to keep it and we carried on southwards. Others, whose cars were confiscated, took out what they could carry and then staggered down the road with incredibly heavy loads. Before long, the weight proved too much and people began to throw things away. We were treated to the amazing sight of discarded bags being snatched up by those behind, only to be discarded once more a few hundred yards down the road as the additional weight became too much for the new owners.

Further on, we watched in astonishment as, horns blowing and flags flying, a convoy of vehicles containing members of the royal family and other VIPs forced their way through the flood of refugees. They drove off boldly towards the south believing that they were safe with the Khmer Rouge because Prince Sihanouk, the former King and then Prime Minister of Cambodia, was now nominally Head of State for the Khmer Rouge regime.

Here and there, people still tried hard to find food which they sold for money. Those without food carefully and sparingly spent what little money remained to them. The old republican currency was the medium of exchange as, even now, no one could believe that it had become valueless. Women took their money and secreted it in long thin bags which they tied around their waists under their clothes. We didn't buy much because Lay's brothers were constantly foraging in nearby orchards and gardens. On one occasion they even managed to catch two pigs. We ate some of the pork immediately with great relish, but preserved most of it for the coming days. Feeling the need to contribute something towards the group, I was still cooking for everyone as I had little else to offer. My culinary abilities began to improve as the days went by.

One hot sticky afternoon, most of us went down to the Mekong River to bathe when the Khmer Rouge were not in sight. I couldn't swim so I hung on to one of the jetty posts, enjoying the cool fresh water of such a large river. The others were swimming a little way from the bank and enjoying themselves for a change when there was a scream and everyone came swimming in a great rush towards the bank.

"What's the matter?" I shouted, getting ready to scramble out quickly myself.

"A corpse is floating in the river," someone replied.

Then I saw it myself, only ten metres away and floating face down away from us. I had had enough of the river and went up to get changed. Somaly didn't want to leave the water just then, so I left her in the care of my younger brother, Peauv. About 20 minutes later, Somaly came up from the river and exclaimed, "Yuk!! . . . I'm not going to eat that any more." There was a look of horror and disgust on her face.

"Eat what?" I asked.

"Lobsters," she replied. "A fisherman at the river caught a lot of lobsters in his net and there were bits of flesh in their claws. I heard people say that the lobsters had eaten the corpses."

This was just one of many incidents which would take place in the years ahead and which would turn my children into adults before their time.

An endless succession of days followed during which our hopes of a return to Phnom Penh slowly evaporated. It seemed almost as if we were moving in a dream world which was rapidly turning into a nightmare. We became more and more exhausted as we trekked southwards. Tempers became frayed and the tension between the two families rose higher until we realised that we had come to a crossroads in our travels together.

It appeared that our family was a constant liability to Lay's family, as we had little to offer in the way of supporting our little community. Our family comprised mainly women and children, whereas Lay's family was made up of strong young men. They were constantly foraging for food and expending energy to feed us. Gradually under such adverse conditions, they began to get fed up and Hear's wife, who used to be very sweet in normal life, became despondent. She resented the way that our family was dragging hers down, as if we were a millstone around their necks. Their words and actions made us realise how unwanted we were, and how much of a liability we appeared to be to them. My brother, An, did his best to contribute his strength and ability to everything they did. However, he was a city man, descended from a middle-class family, and he did not possess the skills and practical abilities of Lay's brothers.

Each night, in my times of quiet when I thanked God for bringing us safely through another day, I asked Him to soften their hearts, so that we might continue to benefit from their help. Hear was a very kind man who proved himself to be a good leader. He couldn't bring himself to cast us away for no reason, but eventually my pride forced me to go to him and say: "I understand your difficulty in staying with us. We are only a burden to you, so please leave us."

This, of course, placed Lay in a very difficult position. He wanted to stay with his own family and yet did not want to be separated from Sokhon. Hear was reluctant to separate anyway and, when Lay added his plea, it was decided to go on together. As there seemed to be no hope of returning to Phnom Penh, we all felt that it would be best to travel on as fast as possible to settle in another town. Lay and his brothers then showed their inventiveness. They soon found an old car and, together, removed the rear axle and part of the chassis. They built a wooden platform on top of it and put four poles in each corner to provide support for a roof made from a strong plastic sheet. To the end of the chassis, they fashioned a tow-bar which they attached to the end of the jeep. There was now sufficient transport for us all. Hear refitted the spark plugs into the jeep which fired immediately. With Hear's family packed into the jeep and our family on the trailer together with the supplies, we set off.

Hear drove slowly along the gravel track, which was dotted with potholes. When it had previously been under government control, the Khmer Rouge had dug it up at night to obstruct the passage of government troops. As Hear zigzagged between the holes, the trailer swung alarmingly from side to side and we hung on for dear life. We draped a piece of canvas above us to ward off the sun and settled down to make the best of it all. It was late afternoon by the time we arrived at the site of a burnt-out village in the middle of the countryside. It was completely deserted and we decided to stay the night as we needed to cook and eat before sunset.

Lay's brothers quickly found two large jackfruits in the abandoned village, and built a large bonfire. Our usual practice had been for all of us to gather round the fire after supper and talk about the past and the future. However, tonight was different and we seemed to separate naturally into two groups sitting silently. Hear's family discreetly ate the jackfruits from which a lovely sweet smell emanated to tickle our taste buds. My mother whispered to me: "I think we should make our own way since the other family seem so unhappy with our presence." I glanced at An, who said: "I think I'll be able to lead us – we'll be all right."

After thinking about it all again, I went across to speak to Hear once more. I began my half-prepared speech. "Thank you for helping us to get half-way to Takeo, but I think the time has come for us to go our separate ways." Hear was very kind and smiled. "Come and eat some jackfruit with us," he invited me. The faces of Lay and his mother fell for they were sad to have this subject raised again so soon. They both knew that it could mean the possible separation of Lay from his own family as he would have to choose whether to accompany Sokhon. The atmosphere was charged with tension and no one seemed willing to discuss it further. Leaving them all to their own thoughts, I rejoined my family to try and sleep. As I settled down and asked God to guide us all in such a difficult decision, I heard the sounds of argument. Hear's wife was arguing with both her husband and her own mother. This made me feel really guilty as I realised that they were having an argument because of us.

In the morning we set off once more. The journey was quiet and strained, with everyone trying to hide their thoughts and emotions. My family was on the trailer again and we wondered about our future. As difficult as life had been since leaving Phnom Penh, it was likely to be much worse without the support of Hear's family. By afternoon we arrived at yet another burnt-out village and stopped for the night. After eating our evening meal of rice, Hear approached me to say that he didn't want to go to Takeo with us as that route appeared to be lined only with empty villages. Also, as Takeo was not a rich area, he preferred to go to Kompong Thom, his family's birthplace, where the land was more fertile. I did not argue with him, but merely nodded, feeling a sense of relief that the tension which had built up between our two families would soon be over. However, a sense of apprehension also struck me – what would be waiting for us at the end of this road?

The next day Hear shared out the rice and other supplies between the two groups. He was very fair and we were grateful to him. As our pile of food, kerosene, cooking equipment and tools grew, we naturally assumed that we would be able to take them all on the trailer, which could be pushed separately from the jeep. However, Hear indicated that he did not want to give up the trailer to us because he felt that he could not fit his whole family and all his supplies into the jeep. Shocked to find that we would be left to carry everything on our own, I pleaded with Hear to give us the trailer. I begged him again and again, but his repeated refusals brought tears to my eyes, and I wept in front of everyone.

After a while, Lay's mother came to speak to my mother and myself. She talked about Sokhon and asked that Sokhon be allowed to go with her family. However, my mother was adamant that she would not allow Sokhon to leave with Lay's family. Lay sat by the roadside looking very sad. We could almost read the thoughts which were battling in his own mind. He was faced with the choice of abandoning his own family or deserting the girl whom he loved.

The whole morning passed with no one able to take such a difficult decision. Lay and Sokhon sat together weeping silently. I was reminded of the verse in the Bible, 'A man shall leave his father and mother and be joined to his wife.' With this in mind, I went to Lay and spoke to him alone. I told him that this was a decision which he would have to make for himself and I reminded him that sooner or later he would have to leave his mother and start his own family. I said that, if he really loved Sokhon, then he should go with her, and that he would be like a brother to me.

Lay pondered on my words for a long time. Suddenly he stood up and walked over to his mother. We didn't know what he was going to say and we waited in silence. One minute . . . two minutes passed. Then his mother burst into tears as she realised that she was losing one of her sons. Lay came over and told us that he was going to accompany us and, without another word, walked to the jeep and unhitched the trailer. His family loaded their supplies into the jeep and, after a tearful farewell, they drove back in the direction of Phnom Penh to find the road to Kompong Thom. We have never heard of them again, and I often wonder whether they were stopped and killed by the Khmer Rouge for the 'crime' of owning and driving a vehicle.

We grieved at the loss of more than half our group, who had been not only our constant support in finding food along the way, but also our only link with the past which we had left behind in Phnom Penh. An and Lay hunted round for a piece of bamboo and, hitching it to the trailer tow-bar, began the long pull towards Takeo.

3   A Thief in the Night

It was already early afternoon, but we knew of another village not very far away at which we hoped to arrive before sunset. While Lay, An and Peauv took it in turns to pull the trailer, the rest of us pushed from behind. Only Panita, who had not yet learned to walk, was allowed to travel on the trailer. As the afternoon progressed, the sun seemed to become hotter and hotter and our pace slower and slower. Every half-hour, we sought out the shade of an overhanging tree and rested for several minutes. After each rest, it became more difficult to drag ourselves to our feet and plod on. It was obvious that we would never reach the village before dark. We had seriously overestimated our ability to travel that far as we were so unused to hauling the trailer.

By 5 p.m. we had begun to look around for a place to spend the night. Already the terrain had changed. Whereas before, the roadside had been dotted with farmers' huts every kilometre or so, now there was nothing but the thick forest reaching down to the road. During the intense fighting from 1970 to 1975, large areas of land had been neglected and the forest had begun to reclaim previously open spaces. As twilight descended upon us, the trees hemmed us in and their shadows, cast by the last dying rays of the sun, stretched out their long menacing fingers towards us.

Before the light completely vanished, we spotted a concrete wall, set back from the road and partly obscured by the foliage. Looking closer, we found the skeleton of a house behind the wall with no roof or walls. A pile of broken bricks lay in the middle. As there seemed no hope of finding anywhere else that night, we decided to stay there. Lay and An found enough wood nearby to make a small fire and we put three small rocks together upon which we could place the cooking pot. It was the first night on our own and, even though there were 11 of us, it seemed very quiet without the other 16 people. The silence plunged us all into a deep sense of sadness. It was already dark by the time we had finished eating. Lay and An stumbled around to hang up our three mosquito nets. It was difficult as there were no convenient poles nearby on which to hang the four corners. In the end they found creepers near the forest edge and used them to lengthen the strings at each corner. Finally the nets were properly hung, the children put to bed on old mats on top of the uneven ground, and the rest of us gathered around the single kerosene lamp.

Our conversation was stilted and intermittent. In the background, and yet close by, we could hear the screeching and clicking of insects. These were normal jungle sounds, but over the air came the eerie call of an owl. It chilled our bones and we huddled closer together. In Cambodia, the owl is thought to be a messenger of evil spirits. The owl's hoot, together with the darkness and our own loneliness, made us afraid. With nothing to talk about and feeling exhausted, we decided to try to sleep. One by one, we wandered off to our nets. An and Lay slept under one net, while Aheng and I slept with Panita and Somaly under another. My mother slept with Sokhon, Da, Srey Vy and Peauv under the third net.

Before joining the others in my net, I picked my way to the edge of the forest to find a spot to relieve myself. As I stood up, a large black form in the shape of a human loomed up in front of me. It was clearly silhouetted against the sky, silent and yet menacing. I started to scream, but fear tightened my throat and no sound came out. Terrified, I ran in the direction of my mosquito net and prayed to God for protection. With the flimsy protection of the net between me and the outside world, I felt somehow safer. Whatever it was had disappeared, and I began to wonder if it had only been my imagination.

I dozed fitfully, only to awake with a start one hour later as Panita screamed. She had not been very well the day before, and now she tossed and turned. Both my mother and Aheng were also awakened and we tried to calm and comfort Panita. However, she became very delirious and began sweating a lot. She quickly vomited up what little food she had in her stomach. Her eyes rolled upwards so that we could only see the whites. I became frantic with worry, but could do nothing except pray silently, asking God to surround my daughter with His loving protection. My mother, who was superstitious, kept throwing small handfuls of our precious supply of rice and salt. Her idea was to provide food for the bad spirit, so that it would be appeased and leave Panita. It seemed to achieve little except to waste our small amount of food.

All three of us were thinking of what we should do to save Panita, but could only rock her to and fro in our arms before putting her down again. I decided to give her a quarter of one of my stomach tablets and apply some tiger balm over her body. It might have been useless to do so, but it was the only thing that I could think of. Every now and then, we fanned her gently with a piece of material. Apart from that, we could only sit and watch the flickering kerosene lamp which I had put on the ground close to the net. As I watched the insects flying into the light, my eyes blurred with tears and I prayed quietly, thanking God for the gift of Panita and asking Him for His healing of her now.

Hours later, the blackness of the night began to recede and the faint light of dawn appeared on the skyline. Panita stirred, breathing more easily, and her skin was cooler to the touch. It was as if God was not only chasing away the night with the light of day, but was also driving away some darker sense of evil which had possessed our campsite during the night.

We all then managed to gain some rest until it became quite light at 6 a.m. Looking around, we caught sight of each other's strained faces and everyone began to speak at once. Somehow we felt that we had to speak out to release the pent-up inner tension. It was apparent that no one had slept well during the night. Mother was the first to relate what she had seen. "I saw a spirit above Panita . . ." I interrupted her before she could go any further. "So that's why you threw away all our precious rice and salt."

Mother replied haughtily: "Yes, and it's thanks to me that Panita is better. I saw an old woman bending over her, asking her to go away with her. If I hadn't thrown the rice and salt to appease her, she would have taken Panita."

Then it was An's turn to speak: "I dreamed that a group of monks walked right through Var's mosquito net." According to Cambodian tradition, dreaming about monks is an indication that an evil spirit is located nearby.

As the light grew stronger, we noticed two recently dug graves not far from where we lay. We had been too busy to notice them when we had arrived the previous evening. Relating my experiences during the night, I added: "I'm not sure what it was, but I am sure that God has protected us all through the night."

Lay felt that it was simply part of our imagination and fear, but we all felt that something unpleasant had been near us throughout our stay there. It didn't take us long to pack up and move out along the trail. We wanted to reach the next village by midday so that we could rest there while the sun was at its hottest.

Upon our arrival, we found over 70 families there already – a few had cars, and they were all camped around the village. We settled down to rest and some peasants came out of the forest carrying palm tree fruit and juice and some coconuts to barter with the city families in exchange for oil, salt, rice, kerosene and clothes. They spoke little and seemed to be afraid of something, as if their contact with us was against the orders of some higher authority.

Leaving that village, we continued to walk and pull our trailer for another week and gradually became more accustomed to the rhythm of moving forward uncertainly carrying all our worldly possessions with us. We had only managed to cover about 40 kilometres when we arrived at the district town half-way between Phnom Penh and Takeo. The rainy season had already begun in earnest and we walked into the village with the rain pouring down. Many other families had arrived in the town and were stuck there sheltering from nature's onslaught.

As it was already evening, we decided that we would stay there as well. The whole area was a sea of mud and, as we slipped and slithered from one part of the town to another, it was apparent that most of the houses had been burned down and destroyed. The area was clearly under the control of the Khmer Rouge and we passed several of them in the streets clad in their black uniforms and clutching their standard-issue AK47 rifles. There was almost nowhere with any shelter from the rain and even the wooden floors, which often were all that remained of the houses, were already occupied. If we had been able to find one of those, at least we would have been able to keep out of the mud.

We stood around in the rain discussing our situation. We were completely soaked through and were faced with the prospect of standing in the rain all night long. It wasn't difficult to come to the conclusion that we might as well continue in the hope of finding somewhere else to stay along the road ahead of us. A Khmer Rouge soldier standing nearby noticed our general air of dishevelment and indecision. He came over and asked us where we wanted to go. We pointed to the Takeo road, but he said that it was impossible to travel very far due to a bridge having been destroyed. It might have been possible to ford the river in daylight, he said, but to have attempted it at night with a trailer and children would have been foolhardy. He suggested that we take another route which ran in the same general direction. It was longer, but safer, he claimed. As we had little choice, we asked him for directions for that route and he began to explain. The thunder of the rain in our ears and our exhausted condition made it difficult for us to understand directions to a road on which we had never travelled before. To our amazement, he suddenly offered to guide us, saying that he intended to travel that particular road himself. Gratefully, we accepted his guidance and followed wearily behind him, the ever-present rifle slung over his shoulder.

We left the town along one of the streets, but as we moved into the countryside the road quickly petered out into a track. The mud was cloying and refused to release our feet. It was impossible to wear any kind of shoes and we all went barefoot. Each step became a battle and we thought only of putting one foot in front of the other. The trailer was almost impossible to handle and slid from side to side of the track. In order to provide a light for everyone to follow, I led the way carrying the kerosene lamp. I could not keep my footing and fell constantly in the mud. I built up a series of bruises all over my body as, each time I fell, I used my body to shield the lamp from breaking. Without its feeble light it would have been impossible to continue. As An and Lay's difficulty in pulling the trailer increased, the Khmer Rouge soldier helped them over the worst patches of mud. We kept thanking him for his kindness and began to form a good impression of the Khmer Rouge in general, especially when he fell over, covering himself with mud, but continued without complaint.

Over the next two hours or so we struggled on and became increasingly exhausted. We passed one or two villages by the side of the track and asked the soldier if there was anywhere there where we could stay. He kept saying that the road would get better in a little while and so we struggled on. My mother was on the point of complete exhaustion and could only walk with the help of Sokhon and Peauv. Da and I took it in turns to hold the lamp and to help Aheng look after Somaly and Panita, while Srey Vy struggled along on her own. Finally, the soldier said that he knew of a village just ahead with a nice pagoda where we could shelter. Immediately, he struck off along a small track leading away from the main trail. For more than half an hour we meandered along the small pathway until I eventually became suspicious and wondered where he was leading us. However, soon after, we arrived at a small village and the soldier led us into the grounds of a pagoda. My suspicions evaporated as we saw that not only was it dry but it also boasted of a well, where we were able to wash the mud off ourselves and scrub our clothes clean.

We had already eaten at 5 p.m. that afternoon but we wanted somehow to show our gratitude to the Khmer Rouge soldier. All we really wanted to do was wash, change and fall into an exhausted sleep. Instead, we got out our cooking equipment and began to cook him a meal of sweetened mung beans. We became even more exhausted as we struggled to light the fire using wet branches which we collected from around the pagoda. Afterwards, we draped our wet clothes around the verandah which surrounded the pagoda. Somehow, our spare clothes in the trailer had remained dry amid the torrential rain, and we thankfully pulled them on. An and Lay gave up their mosquito net for the soldier. As there was no spare mat for An to sleep on, he went to the trailer and lay down on top of all the bags. We all quickly fell into a deep sleep. The strain of dragging ourselves and the trailer through the mud had drained our last reserves of energy.

My mother was accustomed to getting up before anyone else and she arose at 5 a.m. She couldn't see the Khmer Rouge soldier inside his net and thought that he might have left already to go to work. The rest of us woke at 6 a.m. and began to pack our things. The rain had eased during the night and now the sky was clear.

Aheng went out to the verandah to collect some of the clothes. She rushed back asking if I had already taken in all the clothes. We all trooped out to the verandah, one after the other, and stared in amazement at the empty verandah. All the clothes were gone, as well as a sack of old cloth remnants and a large machete. The machete was probably the most serious loss as we needed it to hack our way through the forest along overgrown paths.

Packing up and setting off once more down the small track back to the main trail, we discussed among ourselves about the Khmer Rouge soldier. We realised then why he hadn't let us stop at any other village, but had led us to the empty pagoda where he could rob us without difficulty. We also realised that it was only due to An sleeping in the trailer which had prevented the loss of even more of our supplies. Only one thing puzzled us. Why hadn't the Khmer Rouge man simply robbed us at gunpoint? Could he have been afraid that we would report him, whereas now we had no proof that he was the thief? Or perhaps he was not really Khmer Rouge, but an ordinary peasant disguised as a soldier? Another thought struck me. Perhaps he was really an honest man and, after he left the pagoda, someone from the nearby village came and stole our things. It remained a mystery to us.

Our next stop was at the foot of a hill called Phnom Chiso, where a little village nestled next to a reservoir. It was like leaving a battlefield and entering a place of peace. The area had been under the control of the Khmer Rouge since about 1972 and there was no evidence of destruction. The water in the reservoir was clean and clear. Large lilies and lotuses floated on the surface. A brisk breeze whispered through the leaves of large, shady trees. We felt that we had stepped from a turbulent storm into an oasis of tranquillity. Just to stand under the big shady trees and look at the scene cheered us up.

As we approached the village, we saw that there were queues of people, with their belongings packed in cars and on trailers or piled on bicycles or carts. We were stopped and ordered to join one of the queues which were all being checked by Khmer Rouge soldiers. While waiting, I wandered forward to see what was going on. The Khmer Rouge soldiers claimed to be looking for weapons and ammunition. As each family was searched, they were made to lay out all their belongings on the ground. The Khmer Rouge confiscated any western or modern goods – items which they felt were associated with the former, corrupt society. The women soldiers stacked piles of make-up, jewellery and fashionable clothes, while the Khmer Rouge men piled up watches, radio/cassette recorders, razors, jeans, medicines, tents and rain capes.

It seemed that we were about to be stripped of the last vestiges of our former existence in the name of creating a new society. I walked to a house close by to ask for some water. Inside, I came across a group of Khmer Rouge girls arguing about who should receive which confiscated item. The idealism of pure communism obviously did not extend to these Khmer Rouge. We were not being relieved of our personal effects to prepare us for a new society, but rather to line the pockets of those who now held power with the gun.

Realising that it would not be long before all our things were also stolen in a similar way, I returned to the trailer. Thinking fast, I stopped to ask an old man the name of the Khmer Rouge leader in that area. He told me that the leader's name was Mit Korn.[1] I thanked him and hurried back to the family.

Before long, we were approached by three Khmer Rouge girls and one Khmer Rouge man. "We have to search your things to check for items which are not allowed by the Angkar,"[2] they explained. I replied very politely: "Please go ahead. We are prepared to follow any rules which are laid down by the saviours of our glorious country." As they began to unload the trailer, I continued: "On our way here, we met the District Chief, Comrade Korn, who told us to let our comrade soldiers take anything which is either not safe for us to keep or dangerous to the new society. He only asked us to tell him your names and to make a list of things which you take from us. He was concerned that there had been several complaints of Khmer Rouge soldiers taking things away from the new city people and keeping everything for themselves instead of giving them to the Angkar. Although he doesn't really believe the rumour, he is anxious that the Khmer Rouge should be strictly honest, so that the name of the revolution and of the Angkar can be glorified."

Following my little speech, the Khmer Rouge girls backed away. My insinuation of corruption had hit home and they seemed easily persuaded not to lay hands on our belongings. However, the Khmer Rouge man stood his ground. "Where did you meet Comrade Korn?" he demanded with a disbelieving sneer in his voice. I tried not to let the fear show in my face, while the rest of the family became anxious that my lies would be discovered. I quickly gave the name of the last village through which we had passed and also mentioned that we had a Khmer Rouge soldier as our guide, omitting to mention that we thought he was also a thief.

[1]   In Cambodian, 'Mit' means 'Comrade'.
[2]   'Angkar' is the Cambodian word for 'organisation' and was used widely to refer to the Khmer Rouge leadership.

The man seemed impressed and relaxed his attitude towards us. I was amazed that he had believed me when I said that we had met Mit Korn. It was only a month later that we discovered that Mit Korn darted here and there alone, like a firefly, checking on the Khmer Rouge soldiers' activities. The Khmer Rouge man asked us where we were going to live. I told him that we were aiming for the village of Botrokar, which was only five kilometres from Phnom Chiso, as that was where my aunt and grandmother lived. He asked for their names and, when I told him, he exclaimed that his mother was a good friend of my grandmother. My grandmother used to be a well-known midwife in the area and had delivered almost all of the babies born there. There were big smiles all round when we discovered such close links and the atmosphere eased considerably.

After some further talk, the man told us that we could leave immediately without any confiscations. He requested one shirt for himself as a favour, which I gave to him against An and Lay's will but, at the same time, praising God for our deliverance. We remained at Phnom Chiso for almost two hours to rest in the shade of the trees savouring the cool breeze on our faces.

We set off for Botrokar, which was my mother's birthplace. She had grown up there and had many friends as well as relatives still in the same area. Some of them lived in Phum Slar, a small village just before Botrokar. As we walked through the main street, my mother glanced from side to side, eager to meet some of the people whom she used to know. There were brief glances of recognition and polite greetings before everyone hurried on their way. For my mother, it was a sad home-coming to be greeted so distantly and in such an unfriendly manner.

Arriving in Botrokar, we went straight to my aunt's home. She seemed equally cold and unfriendly and we began to wonder whether we had been wrong to come in the first place. However, it was almost 4 p.m. and we needed somewhere to stay overnight, so she allowed us to remain. To us, it seemed like heaven. It was the first house in which we had stayed peacefully since our expulsion from Phnom Penh nearly a month earlier. There were beds with mats and a proper kitchen, all of which we had missed. Behind the house was a brick retaining wall with steps leading down to a lake, and it wasn't long before we had plunged in to wash off the dust. We shouted cheerfully to each other and, as we played in the water, the tensions of the past month were washed away. At last we were able to enjoy ourselves in what would prove to be a brief interlude of peace.

In such a place it was easy to forget all the horrors that we had experienced. I sat swinging my legs in a hammock behind the house. Delving into my bag, I picked out a book of English poems which I had found along the roadside. Almost as if I had not a care in the world, I began to recite the poems in a rather loud voice, feeling a sense of contentment at being able to practise the English language again. My aunt ran from the house with a look of terror on her face. "Quiet!" she hissed. "Don't you know anything at all? – you city people are so ignorant. I must tell you everything tonight." Rather subdued, I continued to read quietly to myself.

That night we sat around in the house. "What do you plan to do?" my aunt asked us. "We want to go to Takeo where we used to live because some of the other family members may go there to look for us," I replied. My aunt was silent for a while before giving us her advice. "Everything in Takeo has been destroyed in the fighting which took place before the 17th of April. There is nothing there for you to go to."

I didn't particularly want to stay in such a small village and wanted to get back to a town, the ways of which I understood, and so I responded: "I think it is better if we go to Takeo and see what we can find there."

My aunt began to get a little impatient. "It would be better if you stayed in Botrokar, which is peaceful and well organised as it has now been in the hands of the Khmer Rouge for about three years. You are all city people. If you stay here, I will teach you about the Angkar. I have lived among these people for a long time, and I can show you how to behave."

I was still determined to continue, but my mother could see the sense in what my aunt was saying, and she gave the final word. "We will stay for the time being. We can always move on at a later date when we see how the situation develops."

The following morning my aunt led us all to meet the village chief and to have our names registered. We were recorded as 'new' people, which was a term accorded to all those who had been evacuated from the cities. The 'new' people were regarded as being different from the 'old' people, who had already lived under Khmer Rouge control for a number of years. The village chief asked us if we had any food. We answered honestly that we still had one 50 kg sack of rice. The chief seemed kind and said that we should tell him when we ran out and he would give us a new supply.

We were all put to work immediately. Lay, An and Peauv helped to begin the construction of shelters for the 'new' people of the village by sawing wood and collecting bamboo from the forest. Sokhon, Da, Srey Vy and I helped to make roof sections from palm-tree leaves. We laughed together as we learned this new skill and it was a time for relaxed work. As trainees, we were treated well to begin with and it was a welcome break from the days of constantly trudging along the road.

After one week we decided that we would like to continue on our way to Takeo, where my mother owned a large house and two shophouses. We hoped to find them still standing in spite of my aunt's description of the destruction of the town. We felt that we would be able to use the houses to settle down properly and to start a new life. We went to the village chief to obtain his permission to leave, but he said that this was now impossible. We were very disappointed, saying: "Why can't we go on? There are still other people moving along the roads."

The Chief explained: "I have just received orders from Angkar Loeu.[1] All those who have been evacuated from the cities are to stay where they are now. It is now the end of May and it is time to begin planting rice. If everyone continues to wander around the countryside, no rice will be planted. Everyone must learn to be productive in the country and not waste their time in the towns and cities. The Angkar now wants everyone to construct shelters first and then to get on with planting rice. You must all stay in this village and help with the work."

We left him, wondering what our future would be like in such a village. It was so different to the existence to which we were accustomed. As I settled down into the routine of this new type of work, I often lay awake during the night reflecting on my life. My thoughts flew back in time to my early childhood and to the events which had brought me to this point in my life.

---

[1]   Literally, 'Higher Organisation', meaning the *top* Khmer Rouge leadership.

4 My Early Life

I was born on November 9th, 1948, in the provincial town of Takeo. In the late 1940s and early 1950s, Takeo was still an overgrown village which was beginning to mushroom into a town. There was little planning and houses sprang up all over the place. In the centre of the town was a bustling market which started at about 4.30 a.m. each morning. The cries of the vendors echoed around the nearby streets and attracted their first customers as housewives hurried to obtain first choice of the meat, fish, vegetables and fruit that had been brought in from the countryside. Depending on the season, a whole range of colourful fruits were available. 'Hairy' rambutans, a small juicy fruit with white flesh and burrs on the outside skin, nestled next to papayas and mangoes. Pineapples and bananas were much in evidence and my favourite, the mangostein – a round, purple fruit with succulent sections inside – was often to be found.

My mother, Taing Chhaya, had been born and raised in the village of Botrokar about 25 kilometres away. There she had met my father, Hong Yang, who worked drawing up plans for new houses. My first memory is of a small shophouse right in the town centre. My father was not rich, but he was able to rent one long room on top of a bookshop. The room was about 15 metres long and 4 metres wide and ran the length of the house. We partitioned it off with curtains to provide more privacy. Living in a concrete house equipped with electricity and running water, we were luckier than some families.

Although there were a number of Buddhist temples in the town, with gold leaf and ornate carvings, I do not recall being taken there by my parents. However, when I was only about four or five years old, I do remember slipping out of the house every Sunday and toddling along to a nearby building which was used as a church by a small group of Christians in Takeo. It was only 200 metres from our home and was probably the nearest place of excitement apart from the market. I used to stand behind the back row of chairs and peep down the aisle to watch what was going on. There were very few Christians in Cambodia, since the majority of people were Buddhists, and Protestant missionaries had not had a tremendous impact. However, several of the larger towns had a small centre of Christian activity.

I never told my mother where I was going, but would just wander back home after watching for a short while. One Sunday I stayed longer than usual and my mother became worried. Upon returning home, I found her in an angry mood and I was soundly spanked. She told me never to go again.

I was a stubborn child and my mother's injunction only made me more determined to go. The following Sunday I sneaked out of the house and took up my usual position in the church. When the service was over, the realisation of what I had done hit me, and I was afraid to return and face my mother's wrath. Instead, I went off to play with some other children, putting off the fateful time of my return. In the meantime, my poor mother became frantic with worry and sent out various uncles and aunts to search for me. Even my grandfather took up the search, and it was he who found me much later lying asleep under a bush.

My mother, realising what a determined child I was, didn't spank me again. Instead, she told me that I could go whenever I wanted to, as long as I told her first. It was a good compromise.

After I began school at the age of six, I continued to go to the church from time to time. I was attracted at the time by the simple Bible stories that were told. Each time a child was able to recite a few words from one of the Bible stories, he was given a picture from an old Christmas card. To my child's eye, the cards looked incredibly beautiful with their shiny glitter. I struggled hard to remember some of the teaching so that I could earn the lovely cards.

I started school in Takeo when I was six years old, but a few years later we moved to Kompong Thom. My father had joined the Royal Police Force, which was created by Prince Sihanouk after independence in 1954. He gradually rose through the ranks to become a captain, but it meant constant upheavals as he was transferred from Kompong Thom to Kandal and back to Takeo. This second period at Takeo was relatively calm and we began to grow up as a family. All the children were born there. Apart from myself, there were my three younger brothers An, Rathana and Peauv, and my three younger sisters Sokhon, Da and Srey Vy. When I was 17, I took and passed my *Diplôme d'Études Secondaires*, which is equivalent to about ten 'O' levels. I went on studying but unfortunately failed my baccalaureate exam.

With my father becoming a fairly prominent policeman, it was natural that I should develop the ambition of following in his footsteps. However, my grandfather was very keen that I should become a teacher and eventually I succumbed to his influence. I went away to Kandal Province to attend the Teacher Training College for two years.

Newly qualified, I returned to Takeo to teach in a primary school. It was there that I met once again the man who would become my husband, Lach Virak Phong. I had first met him when my father had hired him five years earlier to give me special tuition in maths. He was now a senior teacher as well as being commissioner of the youth movement in Takeo. He rented one of the shophouses nearby which belonged to my mother, and our romance quickly flourished. It was not long before he summoned the courage to approach my father and ask for my hand in marriage. The wedding, a traditional Cambodian affair, was scheduled to take place a few months later in 1968. Since I was the eldest daughter and the first one to be married, it turned out to be a large gathering. Almost a thousand people came from far and wide to attend the ceremonies at different times over a period of three days. In the afternoon of the last day, the monks from the nearby Buddhist temple came to preside over the proceedings and to bless our marriage.

We spent a happy two months together before Virak Phong had to leave for India to do six months' regional training. My sadness at our parting was soon replaced by a growing excitement as I realised that I was pregnant. I continued to teach at school until Virak Phong returned from India. As it was drawing close to the time to deliver the baby, I took maternity leave from my government teaching post and we moved to Phnom Penh. Not long afterwards, on March 23rd, 1969, I gave birth to a beautiful daughter with whom we were delighted. According to our family custom, Virak Phong's father chose the name for our baby. He named her Somaly, which means 'Garland of Flowers'. We were very pleased because she was as lovely to us as any flower.

After some time, I went back to teaching at school in Phnom Penh while Somaly was looked after during the day by a nanny. I looked forward each day to returning home and seeing the changes in her. Several months later, she suddenly fell sick. Our doctor advised us that she needed some sea air to help her become stronger, and we sent her with her nanny to stay with my aunt who was living in my father's chalet in Kep, a Cambodian sea-side resort in Kampot Province. Each weekend Virak Phong and I travelled the 180 kilometres from Phnom Penh to visit her. Kep was a beautiful little town with a lovely atmosphere. It was still very much a Cambodian resort and had not yet been invaded by too many foreign tourists. There were several golden beaches lined with palm trees. The cool breeze from the sea was refreshing and, within a few months, Somaly was sufficiently better to be able to return and live with us in Phnom Penh.

Over the next three years, Virak Phong was in and out of Cambodia as he was sent first to Australia for English training, then to India for a seminar and finally to Japan for further study, where I was able to join him for a short while. Between his trips abroad, Virak Phong worked as a statistician for the Ministry of Education in Phnom Penh, but upon his return from Japan he was appointed as a political advisor to the army with the rank of major. Sihanouk's fall in 1970, and the subsequent increase in Khmer Rouge activity, had meant that almost every able-bodied man was required to help stem the advance of the communists out of the mountains and jungles. Virak Phong was based in the front line in Takeo Province under my uncle, General Kong Chhath, who was governor of Takeo Province.

While teaching at the primary school in Phnom Penh, I often took Somaly along with me. She was eager to learn and, even as a four-year-old, she led the class of six-year-olds whom I taught each day.

Our second child was born on October 8th, 1973, and my father named her Panita, which means 'Good Wife'. Virak Phong returned at the same time to live and work in Phnom Penh. I had been steadily training as an English teacher over a period of two years at the *Faculté de Pédagogie* in Phnom Penh. As part of my training I carried out teaching practice at the Khmero-Anglais High School and Toul Kauk High School.

In the middle of 1974 Virak Phong was given the opportunity by UNESCO to go to Paris and finish his training at the International Institute of Educational Planning. It was an opportunity not to be missed since he would then qualify as an educational planning expert. He left us in August 1974 for a year's training. As we waved goodbye to him, none of us realised that the war and the Khmer Rouge would separate us so soon.

One day, not long after Virak Phong had left, I was returning from school to our house in the Toul Kauk suburb of Phnom Penh when I passed a house with a sign in English outside. It read 'Summer Institute of Linguistics'. I was anxious to improve my spoken English and I reasoned that a house for linguistics must have an English speaker. I rang the bell and a western lady came to the door. I explained in English that I was looking for someone with whom I could practise my English. I was invited in and discovered that she was called Rosalyn and was from Australia. She had been looking for someone to teach Khmer to her friend, Barbara, who was due to arrive in two months' time from Vietnam. I was keen to improve my English and I asked if I could pop in from time to time while waiting for her friend, Barbara, to arrive. Rosalyn agreed and I made some delightful visits there – sometimes playing table-tennis and sometimes just chatting.

I was not very clear about what the Institute was doing in Cambodia, nor was I very interested at the time. However, Rosalyn explained to me that the Summer Institute of Linguistics was a Christian organisation that had set itself the task of translating the Bible into the different languages of the world, so that everyone would have the opportunity to read it.

The school holidays arrived and I decided to find additional ways of improving my spoken English. A friend of mine, Mrs Mam I, worked for Catholic Relief Services as a food distribution supervisor, and she often spoke to me about how good the Christian relief agencies were in helping the Cambodians. Mam I's conversations with me made me want to see for myself how good they really were. Many of the relief agencies were run by Christians, carrying out relief activities in war-torn Cambodia. They were involved in emergency food distribution activities, medical care and supplementary feeding for malnourished children. Another friend of mine was the personnel manager for the World Vision relief agency and, when one evening I was invited to his house for dinner, I boldly asked him if he had any vacancies during my school holidays. As I was willing to work as a volunteer, I was eventually given a position as an interpreter in the World Vision Child Care Centre in Toul Kauk.

On my first day there, I was tremendously impressed with the way in which the babies were cared for. I thought to myself how much more caring the Christians were to others – in fact much more so than ourselves. I threw myself into the work enjoying the opportunity to practise my English, but also enjoying the opportunity to be part of a team caring for the many sick children who came to the centre.

A week after beginning work, I began to notice that the other Khmer staff seemed particularly cold towards me. I was baffled by their obvious reluctance to talk to me and, one day, I cornered the cook in the kitchen. She was generally more talkative than the others and I thought I might be able to discover from her the reason why everyone seemed to be avoiding me. She seemed reluctant to say anything, but I kept pressing her. Eventually she replied: "Look, if you don't feel welcome, why don't you stop working here?"

I felt somewhat shocked by her bluntness, which bordered on being very rude, so I immediately asked her if she was a Christian, since I had been told that most people who worked there were Christians. When she replied affirmatively, I said: "Christian people should not be so rude."

The cook was obviously affronted, but began to open up. "Christians are not supposed to lie either, so I will tell you. Nobody likes you because they think you are a government spy." The accusation almost left me speechless, but I blurted out: "What on earth makes them think so?" The cook replied: "No one works for nothing."

I realised then that my volunteer status, which was simply to improve my English, had turned the other staff against me. They had not understood that I was only on holiday from my regular job as a teacher, and had reasoned to themselves that no one could afford to work for no money, unless they were in the pay of the government.

I went on working there for another week, but the atmosphere of icy indifference continued. I wanted to stay on, but I felt that I was in the way of the other staff all the time. It became too difficult and I stopped working there.

However, I continued with my regular visits to Rosalyn, who had now been joined by Barbara. She had been in South Vietnam before as a missionary and was eager to learn Khmer. We got on well together and eventually she asked me if I would accompany her to church each Sunday to translate the sermons which were preached in Khmer and to put her in touch with other Cambodians.

I recalled my childhood visits to the church in Takeo and also my recent experiences of Christian care for the Khmer children in Toul Kauk. I was interested to see what the Christian gospel was all about, so I agreed to go. The following Sunday we went to a church called Maranatha, which was run by an American couple, Todd and DeAnn Burke.[1]

As I sat in the church with my two foreign friends, I felt embarrassed and even wanted to laugh out loud at times. I watched in amazement as people prayed, closing their

---

[1]   Authors of *Anointed for Burial*.

eyes and lifting their hands high in the air. They burst into song joyously, singing from their hearts. They seemed strange, almost set apart from other Cambodians whom I knew. The only logical explanation, I said to myself, was that they were all crazy.

However, I enjoyed Barbara's company and I wanted to continue teaching her Khmer and improving my English. So I went regularly to the church each Sunday, interpreting the message that was preached and helping Barbara to make new friends.

I could not sit and interpret without listening to, and trying to understand, the sermons myself. There was a different message each week, but the central theme revolved around what the life of Jesus Christ meant to the individual. It was not some theoretical list of dos and don'ts which was often the centre of other religions. The people who spoke each week seemed to be saying that the Spirit of Jesus could live within each individual and make him a better person. Gradually, I began to link the Christian message with the actions of the Christian relief agencies which I had witnessed. The Christians working for the agencies demonstrated a love for the people whom they were helping, and this was similar to the love which God showed and showered on each person who turned to Him.

Through Barbara, I came to meet many other Christians and found them to be 'normal' people, who were filled with a strange kind of happiness. The joyful abandonment in the church, demonstrated by the singing and lifting of hands, was their way of praising God and seemed a complete contrast to the solemnity of the Buddhist temples which I had occasionally visited.

Eventually, I came to realise that the Christians were trying to act in the way that the Bible told them to in order to become more Christlike and were not just paying lip-service to a set of rules and regulations. There was another aspect of Christianity which struck me. This was the ability of Christians to communicate on an individual basis with God. Unlike Buddhism, where prayers consisted of set chants and incantations, the prayers of the Christians were spontaneous and relevant to their daily lives. They gave thanks for His care for them, they confessed their faults and they brought their problems to Him, asking for His help.

The Buddhist contrast with Christianity became clearer to me several weeks later, when my mother invited a monk to our home to give a blessing. The monk spoke of all the money which various rich people had given him to build a shrine within the temple grounds, but neglected to mention the poor people who had also contributed to the appeal. His emphasis on large donations was designed to impress my mother and to encourage her to give a similar large gift. I wondered why there was no mention of assistance to poor people in the area, since that would have been of more use than the building of yet another shrine. Buddhism teaches that the size of the gift is unimportant – it is the desire to give which counts. The message of the monk seemed to be clear – the more money we donated to the temple, the better chance we would have of eventually going to heaven.

I knew, from listening to the messages in the church, that the Christian religion did not judge a person's value by how much money he gave or by his wealth on earth. I recalled a verse from the Bible which I had heard in church: "Don't store up treasures here on earth, where they can erode away or be stolen. Store them in heaven, where they will never lose their value." Some actions, such as spending money on oneself or on making oneself look good in the eyes of others, would be left behind. However, little actions of kindness would be remembered and were more likely to be of credit in heaven.

I knew that the Buddhist temples around Cambodia were tremendously useful within society. They provided schools, particularly in the rural areas where the government was unable to do so. They also looked after students who couldn't find other lodgings. In ways such as this, they seemed to fill a vitally needed social function, but it seemed to me that there was something missing within their religious concept. Although the temples provided physical help for certain people, there was a spiritual need which could not be filled. The more I thought about it, the more I realised that there was a gap in my life which could not be filled by Buddhism. I became determined to find out more and to see if Christianity perhaps had the answer.

One Sunday at church, the first song to be sung was "Seek ye first the Kingdom of God, and all these things shall be added unto you". For the first time the meaning of the words struck home to me. I realised at last that the Kingdom of God began here on earth within my heart and that Jesus was a person who could become real to me. As I knelt in the church, I asked Jesus to enter into my life. There was no dramatic explosion of light in front of my eyes, but there was a sense of peace as if I had reached a watershed in my life.

I went home with the song ringing in my ears and I kept humming the tune. My mother greeted me as I went in and asked me what I was humming. I explained, expecting her to be angry, but she didn't seem put out. I had often told her about the things which I heard at the church and about the Christians doing so many good things to help our people in their time of need. I think, perhaps, that that was why she didn't react angrily towards me for having something to do with Christianity. Emboldened by her seemingly cooperative attitude, I decided to press her further. "What would you think if I became a Christian?" I asked her.

She answered me with her own question: "Why do you want to become a Christian?"

I told her of my experience in the church and of my

decision to ask Jesus into my life. Although I explained my understanding of the difference between Buddhism and Christianity, I expected strong opposition from my mother, who had been a devout Buddhist all her life.

I was amazed that she had almost no reaction to my arguments, but she simply said: "It's up to you what you do, but I think you should ask your husband first."

I wrote immediately to Virak Phong in France, telling him of my feelings and asking for his endorsement for me to become a Christian. Although he was a wonderful husband and had allowed me to do much as I pleased, I wrote without much hope as his family were very strongly-committed Buddhists. I did not think it likely that he would consent to me discarding our country's religion and assuming another.

I had underestimated the power of God. Two weeks later I received Virak Phong's reply. He simply wrote that it was up to me if I wanted to become a Christian, but that he would discuss it with me further when he returned to Cambodia. I was stunned by the reaction of both my mother and my husband. For them to give their consent for me to become a Christian was almost unbelievable. I realised that God was already at work in my life.

I decided to be baptised just before Christmas, 1974. I made arrangements with the Maranatha Church and arrived there early on the Sunday morning. I was not the only one being baptised and several other people also joined me in the simple ceremony. Todd, the pastor, sprinkled water on our foreheads and made the sign of a cross as he welcomed us into the family of Christ. It signified that we now belonged to Christ and was a moving occasion for me.

Although Buddhism was interwoven into the fabric of Cambodian life, I was not particularly aware of any tension at the time between Buddhism and Christianity. Because of the poor state of the economy, rampant inflation and the civil war that was tearing the country apart, people thought more about themselves and their own welfare than about religious differences. In addition, even though I had made the decision to become a Christian, I still attended various festivals and celebrations, such as weddings, funerals and traditional ceremonies, where monks from the nearby temple were invited to officiate and to give their blessings. This was considered a part of the Cambodian way of life and did not necessarily mean that one was a Buddhist. For me, my participation meant only that I was a Cambodian and did not signify the worship of Buddha.

Meanwhile, the general situation on the military front against the Khmer Rouge was beginning to deteriorate. The communists were gaining control of more and more of the countryside and many refugees flooded into Phnom Penh. With the population of the capital more than doubled, the government decided that children should only attend school half-time so that all the extra children could be catered for. For me, it meant that I only taught in the mornings. In the afternoons I was free to do as I wished, and I set up a small sales business. I acted as a general agent to assist in the sale of houses, pieces of land, cars and different types of jewellery. I enjoyed the opportunity to work very much, and it afforded me the possibility of earning some extra money to help take care of my family. The value of the Cambodian Riel was virtually nothing as inflation had taken hold of the economy and the government simply printed more money.

My new-found faith gave me courage in the face of the growing war. Each evening I spent time in prayer, giving thanks for the way in which my needs were taken care of. The absence of my husband was often a cause of concern, but we had good news of him as he studied in Paris.

Before long the Khmer Rouge were pressing closer to Phnom Penh and they began to fire rockets into the outer suburbs. Toul Kauk was an obvious target, and the Khmer Rouge aimed for the police barracks which were situated close to my house. At the beginning only a few rockets fell in our area, and refugees crowded in from the countryside. They put up temporary shelters in the roads and on the pavements. Some built little shacks along our fence and came to us to collect water.

Soon the intensity of the rockets increased, and we were forced to dig an underground shelter. We laid thick tree trunks across the top and covered those with sand bags, leaving only a small entrance. As the number of rockets coming into Toul Kauk increased, so we spent most of our time outside our house in the garden. We cooked and sat under the shade of a large tree not far from the underground shelter. We could hear the rockets coming in as they whistled through the air and we soon came to recognise their special whine. Once we heard that noise, we knew that we had only about four seconds to get into the shelter. Many times during the day we heard the rockets, and it became routine for us to dive into the shelter in a tangle of arms and legs.

Only twice did rockets come very close to our home. The first time, in March, a rocket landed only 50 metres away just outside our garden. It exploded right on top of a refugee house and two people were killed instantly, with several others wounded. The second rocket landed about 100 metres away, but only killed a pig and slightly wounded a few people.

We knew that sooner or later some of us would be killed or injured if we stayed, since more and more rockets were starting to shower our area. It was at that point that we were invited to stay with Lay's family right in the city centre, and so we packed our bags and moved out of our home, leaving only Rathana with his books.

5 "We will review your case tomorrow"

My thoughts of the past returned to the reality of the present in the village of Botrokar. The surrounding countryside was in stark contrast to the built-up areas of Phnom Penh to which we had become accustomed. Around the village, the land was flat and consisted of rice paddy fields stretching one after the other into the distance. In one direction we could see the small mountain of Phnom Chiso, while in the other direction, even further away, was another mountain. Small clumps of trees dotted the landscape amongst the paddy fields. The rains were just beginning and the dry brown earth was already starting to yield its green finery as the water performed its life-giving work. Soon, the rains would begin in earnest and the skies would open as torrential rain thundered down for half an hour or an hour at a time. As quickly as they started, the rains would stop and the sun would come out to dry the ground, giving rise to steamy clouds and increasing the humidity in the air. No more electric fans or air-conditioners to keep cool with – we had to put up with the heat and the sweat which trickled down our faces. There were no more occasions to go out to restaurants and to sit quietly talking with friends or to dance together while listening to music. Instead, we had to get used to living in cramped wooden huts and working in the fields, without weekends or holidays, under the watchful supervision of our new masters.

Life began calmly enough and we started to settle into a routine as everyone became more organised. Young boys were detailed off to take care of the cattle, while the small girls either cleaned out the cattle pens or were sent off to collect the cattle dung for use as fertiliser. Each day the men and women went off to dig huge reservoirs and irrigation canals in preparation for the rains which were already beginning. In my group there were about 500 people and we were engaged in digging a reservoir. At the beginning I enjoyed myself and worked hard. It was a relief to be away from the war and to be involved in practical work. In contrast to the shattered buildings in the cities and towns, the countryside held an air of excitement and it was always interesting for me to discover new things.

When we realised that we could not go on to Takeo, the whole family set their minds to staying on, but we retained the hope that we would eventually be allowed to leave the village. Everyone was asked to work except for my mother, who stayed home to look after Somaly and Panita since Aheng had been ordered by the Khmer Rouge to go and join her family. My mother was not properly recovered from her operation and she was beginning to experience pain in her eyes.

Mother also felt that it was time to do something formally about the relationship between Lay and Sokhon. Since neither the Khmer Rouge nor the circumstances would permit a traditional wedding, my mother and aunt organised a small family ceremony with some of the food we had brought with us from Phnom Penh. My mother lit a candle and a few incense sticks and announced that Lay and Sokhon had become husband and wife. Tears welled up in my mother's eyes and fell to the ground. We were all a little sad since it should have been an exciting time for everyone. In normal circumstances, there would have been a large gathering to celebrate their wedding. I remembered my own wedding day and thought of the difference. On the other hand, I was happy for Lay and Sokhon that they had each other during these difficult times. After Mother's little ceremony, we ate a simple meal to celebrate the addition of Lay to our family.

For the first weeks of our stay in the village, we still had some food and other supplies left, so life didn't seem too bad. The Khmer Rouge seemed to be patient in their attempts to educate us and teach us how to live like peasants. Although we missed our former life, our present situation left us with no choice, and we were thus able to accept the new life style.

My day began at 5 a.m. when I got up to cook the midday meal which we carried with us to the fields. By 6 a.m. we were already at work and we finished between 5 and 6 p.m. with an hour's break for lunch in the middle of the day. When we had finished digging reservoirs and irrigation canals, we were all sent into the fields to help with the rice planting. The men tilled the fields using cows and buffaloes to pull the ploughs, while the women planted the rice seed in small paddy plots ready for transplanting later to the ploughed fields. While we waited for the seedlings to grow before we could transplant them, the women were ordered to handhusk existing stocks of rice, which were then stored for later consumption. The men worked to produce new ploughs and to build new ox-carts.

Gradually life began to get harder and it was as if the Khmer Rouge were slowly applying pressure to train us. Twice a week, everyone in the village was called to a meeting called 'Kor Sang' – meaning 'a time of constructive criticism'. Whenever the Khmer Rouge spotted us doing something wrong, they said nothing at the time, almost lulling us into a false sense of security. Then, at the next Kor Sang, we were faced with our errors and forced to confess our faults publicly, promising never to do it again. We came to dread the twice weekly meetings, wondering what new thing we would be blamed for.

To begin with, I didn't understand the gravity of the situation in which I found myself. Whenever I wanted to talk to a friend of mine without anyone else understanding, I used to speak in English or French. It was not long before we were overheard by a Khmer Rouge soldier and, at the next Kor Sang, we were accused of supporting the reactionary forces. We had to stand and publicly confess our faults. It was a humiliating experience, but it served to put me on my guard and to make me careful of what I said.

As the work intensified, and we needed all the energy we could get, the food ration was reduced to one condensed milk-tin of rice per person per day plus one spoonful of salt per family per day. It seemed scarcely enough to fill the gnawing hunger in our bellies. Everyday during the lunch hour, people swarmed into the paddy fields to catch small fish, crabs, snails, frogs – in fact anything which moved was much sought after to supplement our meagre diet of rice and salt.

By July the rains had begun in earnest and the paddy fields became gorged with water. We were sent out to pull up the young rice plants from the seed plots ready for transplanting. We tied the plants into bunches and left them for the men to carry to the freshly ploughed fields. I was unused to such hard back-breaking work and, at the end of each day, I ached all over. At times I felt as if I had been physically beaten, and I wandered home from the fields in an absolute daze.

The practice of pulling up the young rice plants was one way in which the original villagers of Botrokar could inflict a bizarre form of torture on those of us who had come from Phnom Penh. In order to prepare the plants for transplanting and to make them light enough for carrying to the paddy fields, the clump of soil clinging to the plant roots had to be shaken off. The most effective method of achieving this was to clutch the plant in both hands and, raising one leg from the water, to beat the plant against the side of one's foot. The soil came off immediately. From years of practice, the farming women were able to pull the plant in such a way that a large lump of mud clung to the roots. Then, taking careful aim at the Phnom Penh women, they hit the plant against their foot, sending a ball of mud into our faces. It was extremely painful, but we dared not retaliate for fear of reprisals from the Khmer Rouge. At the end of each day, we went home covered in mud and smarting from the continual barrage.

One day, one of the women who had come from Phnom Penh, but who had grown up in the countryside, could not bear this cruelty any longer and retaliated by lobbing lumps of mud in a similar fashion at some of the 'old' people. The poor woman was immediately attacked by all the others. We were powerless to help since they were more numerous than us and we were afraid that they would turn on us next. It was a painful scene of which to be a part.

Now my day began at 4 a.m., when I got up to cook rice, and I began work at 5 a.m. It was still dark as we trudged out to the fields and I numbly followed in the footsteps of those ahead of me. Our lunch break was reduced to half an hour and I often had no energy to go into the paddy field in search of extra food. As the day drew to an end and the sky darkened at 6 p.m., we headed home to the village for our evening meal. Even then, we were not allowed to rest. At 8 p.m. the Khmer Rouge drove us out to the fields again to continue working until 11 p.m. Sometimes we were forced to continue until 2 a.m. in the morning, pulling up the young rice plants under the feeble light of the moon ready for planting the next day. The Khmer Rouge leader sat in the corner of the field with a kerosene lamp directing operations. In the darkness it was difficult to see and occasionally, instead of grasping the rice plants, a woman would take hold of a snake. A terrified scream then pierced the night air and confusion reigned for several minutes. The snakes were not poisonous and no real harm was done. Fortunately, there were few of the black, blood-sucking leeches in that area, which saved us a great deal of worry.

Although the work was difficult, we slowly became used to it. As a family we worked hard at the different tasks to which we were assigned and this was noted and occasionally remarked on by some of the Khmer Rouge. In one Kor Sang, the Deputy Chief of the village, a real hard-core Khmer Rouge woman who had been trained in Hanoi, announced that she really appreciated my family. Among all the people who had come from Phnom Penh, she felt that we were the ones who really wanted to change and to follow the Angkar. Her announcement surprised us, but it was a relief to know that we stood in some degree of favour with the Khmer Rouge.

When the rice ration was decreased and our original store of food from Phnom Penh was depleted, I began to worry about the children. Because my mother, Somaly and Panita did not work at that time, they were considered as non-productive members of the village and were only given half a milk-tin of rice a day. This was not enough to survive, especially for children whose growing bodies cried out for protein and nourishment. Meanwhile, the Khmer Rouge had more than enough to eat and we could often see them eating a ration much larger than ours. I began to look around for ways to add to our food supplies.

After making discreet enquiries, I found a Khmer Rouge woman who was willing to sell off some of her excess rice. When we had fled from Phnom Penh, I had taken with me my small amount of jewellery, which I had kept hidden away for a rainy day. Now I carefully selected a small piece of gold and sent Somaly to rendezvous with the Khmer Rouge woman to whom I had already spoken. Somaly soon returned with the extra rice which could mean the difference between living and dying for her and Panita. Each day, Somaly surreptitiously brought back an extra kilogram of rice, which we kept in a small sack and every day we would dip into our precious store of extra rice so that the children could have enough to eat. It was dangerous because the Khmer Rouge had forbidden the purchase of extra food, considering that the ration was quite adequate for those who worked. Those who didn't work through being too young, too old or sick were considered non-productive and therefore of no use to the new society.

The village houses were built on stilts and we had been assigned to live under one of the houses occupied by the leader of a Khmer Rouge women's group. A month after acquiring our extra rice, she noticed that we were cooking and eating more than our ration, and she went immediately to report me to the village chief. The following morning a Khmer Rouge man came to tell me not to go to work. I guessed immediately that something was wrong, but I wasn't sure what. While everyone else went off to the fields, I waited at home worrying.

At 8 a.m. two Khmer Rouge informers (or spies), called 'chhlop', came into the house and, without a word, went directly to the place where I stored my rice. They collected the rice and took it away, but I was too frightened to protest or to say anything. Half an hour later, another chhlop came by and ordered me to accompany him to the house of the village chief. I had no idea what the outcome would be, but I knew that others had been taken away for similar 'crimes'. In some cases, the 'criminals' were severely punished by being forced to work without food or by being tied up and left in the burning sun. In other cases, the Khmer Rouge had taken the person into the forest and had beaten him to death with a blow to the back of the head.

As I walked towards the village chief, I prayed to God for deliverance. There was nothing that I could do to save myself. Approaching the house, I saw the chief sitting down with a large stick and a coil of rope beside him. I recognised them immediately as weapons which the Khmer Rouge used to torture or to kill those who had broken their rules, and I felt a cold chill down my back. With a thudding heart, I began to worry about who would look after Somaly and Panita when I was dead. Once again, I felt waves of guilt crushing me down because I had not made a better effort to take the children to join my husband in France before the Khmer Rouge takeover.

As I stared at the weapons of death, my face paled and I began to tremble. My legs seemed to be made of jelly and I sank down on to the ground in front of the chief. He questioned me harshly and I answered him honestly in a shaky voice about my reasons for obtaining extra rice.

"Why did you buy rice with gold?" he questioned me in a hard voice. "You know that this is against the rules of the Angkar. You are trying to rebel. Haven't you yet learned your lesson? The Angkar allows each person to have one tin of rice every day. You have shown great disrespect to the rule of the Angkar."

All I could manage to say was, "Yes, I confess my fault." My only hope lay in ingratiating myself, and I continued: "I promise to improve myself according to the Angkar's wonderful rules."

The village chief saw that I was pale and trembling and said: "Well, we have to treat you the same as anyone else. The Angkar treats people equally."

This doubled my fright and I waited for the pronouncement of the punishment. Before he could say anything else, a chhlop came up and whispered in his ear. The chief was silent for a few moments, and then he turned back towards me. I expected him to order me to follow the chhlop who would take me away for execution.

Instead, he said, "We will review your case tomorrow. I have something important to do now." Relief flooded over me and I felt happy because I would be able to see my mother and daughters for one more night. However, I fully expected to die the next day.

Returning home, I explained to my mother what had happened. She was overjoyed to see me again, but the children greeted me as normal, not understanding what was wrong. That night, I couldn't sleep. My mother prayed for me according to her Buddhist beliefs, and then proceeded to remind me that I was a Christian and should pray hard to God. How amazing that my own mother, a staunch Buddhist, should remind me of where to look for deliverance! I spent the night asking God for His help in the situation and placing myself in His care. Before Somaly fell asleep, I took the opportunity to explain to her about Jesus Christ and about my faith in God. I wanted her to begin to understand and to also place her trust in Him.

At 4.30 a.m. my mother came to wake me and I quickly cooked the rice, packing it ready for an early departure. As the first group of villagers left for the fields, I ran to accompany them. While everyone else concentrated on planting the young rice plants, I kept glancing towards the path which led back to the village. Each time that I saw a man striding along the path towards where we were working, I thought to myself, "This is it – he's coming to get me." My legs went weak again and I had no energy. By the end of the day I was completely exhausted and emotionally drained of strength. I remembered the incident at a Kor Sang when the Deputy Chief of the village had noted her appreciation of my family's hard work. Could it be possible that she had persuaded the village chief to give me another chance?

The next two days passed with nothing happening, but whenever I was approached by a chhlop or by one of the Khmer Rouge, fear struck deep into my heart. Each evening, I gave thanks to God for allowing me to live for one more day. Gradually my fears subsided and, after one week, I began to feel safe. It seemed amazing that the village chief had forgotten all about my case and I thanked God for saving me.

From then on, I worked twice as hard, but life in the village had lost its sense of novelty. I no longer wanted to stay there but preferred to go elsewhere and make a new start. One day I heard that the Khmer Rouge were gathering all the teachers in Takeo Province into one village somewhere in the middle of the forest. I felt that this would be a chance not only to make a fresh start, but also to locate some of my friends who were teachers. Going straight to the village chief, I asked for his permission to transfer to the new village in the forest. He already knew that I was a teacher and readily gave his permission.

A few days later, the leader of the chhlop came to me and said: "Even though you have permission from the village chief to go to the new village, don't go."

I was amazed at this and immediately demanded: "Why not?" He would only reply: "I feel for your family" – and with that cryptic remark, he walked away.

I was very annoyed that he was blocking me in my attempt to leave the village, but something in his face told me that he didn't intend any harm to me. I decided to wait. Two months later a rumour passed through our village. It seemed that, at the teachers' village, a Khmer Rouge jeep came from time to time and took away a group of teachers. They were never seen or heard from again and it was widely believed that they had been killed.

Once again, I gave thanks to God for his second deliverance from danger, marvelling that He was able to use even a chhlop to save me. After that, whenever I used the foot-pounder to dehusk rice, which was located next to the house of the chhlop chief, a hand was thrust through the grass thatch wall of his house. Each time I was astounded to see an offering of a small amount of cooked rice in the hand, which must have belonged to the leader of the chhlop. Truly God worked in mysterious ways to keep me alive.

Even though I was a relatively young Christian, I was glad that I had spent time before the fall of Phnom Penh studying my Bible. Now certain verses came back to my mind to encourage me in these difficult circumstances. There was no opportunity for me to meet with other

Christians as no one would have dared admit to being a Christian. However, I continued discreetly to tell Somaly about my faith with reference to the parts of the Bible that I could remember.

Work continued in the village. After the rice was all planted, we were sent to the mountain of Phnom Chiso to collect stone. We walked the five kilometres with no shoes and under the hot sun, carrying the stone in a basket on our heads. By working hard, I began to be appreciated once more by the Khmer Rouge authorities. However, the hard work took its toll on my health and my stomach problem returned. Before long, I was too sick to work and I had to stay at home. My fear of the Khmer Rouge increased my worry, because I knew how much they hated people who didn't work. It was already December and the days were becoming cooler. The nights were quite cold and I shivered underneath an old piece of sacking trying to keep warm.

Almost overnight my worry turned to mounting excitement as a rumour swept the village that we were going to be transferred to Battambang Province, which lay 600 kilometres to the north-west of Botrokar. Before long the rumour was confirmed and the Khmer Rouge told us that we were being transferred because the soil in Battambang was much richer and would produce better crops of rice.

Eventually the day of departure arrived and the Khmer Rouge called us together in the evening to tell us that we had to walk to the railway station, which was about 30 kilometres away. We had barely 48 hours to get there as the train was scheduled to depart in two days' time. That evening the village was agog with excitement as everyone hurried to pack their belongings. With 30 kilometres to walk and our possessions to carry, we wanted to make as early a start as possible. No one in the village knew what awaited us in Battambang, but we were overjoyed at the thought of going there. We all knew that Battambang was the richest province in Cambodia and that food was more easily available. There often used to be two crops of rice and its proximity to the large lakes of Tonle Sap meant that fish was abundant.

However, amid the joy, a shadow of gloom lay over my own family. My brother, An, lay sick in the village clinic, which was a simple straw hut with one long bamboo bed lining one wall, where the patients lay next to each other. It was run by Khmer Rouge 'doctors' who were uneducated and had no training in western techniques. There were no medicines or medical equipment in the clinic and the doctors used traditional herbal remedies to try and heal the sick.

An had been sick for several months and had only been able to work for the first few months of his stay in the village. His body was grotesquely swollen and his skin had turned yellow. He was too weak to walk and barely had strength to stand up on his own. How could we hope to carry him 30 kilometres to the railway station? Yet we could not bear the thought of leaving him behind to almost certain death.

I went immediately to the Khmer Rouge village chief to ask for permission to take An out of the clinic. He sent me to ask the chief chhlop, who sent me back to the Village Chief. Throughout that night and the following morning, Sokhon and I went from one person to another to get permission, but no one was willing to make a decision. We wept at the frustration of it all. By midday, many people had already left the village on their way to the railway station and my family was becoming desperate. We saw An stumble out of the clinic hut and sit by the gate watching other people leave. Tears poured down his face as he anticipated being left behind on his own. My mother went over to comfort him and we all followed. Soon we were all crying, kneeling on the ground and begging the clinic chief to let An go.

It came to the point where I was almost certain that the

Khmer Rouge would not allow An to leave. I didn't want him to see me crying, so I went away to find a quiet place to pray, and to ask for God's protection for An.

"Lord, if it's Your will for him to stay here, give me the strength to bear it and to go on looking after the rest of the family," I prayed in a faltering voice. "But if it's right that he should come with us, then soften the hearts of the Khmer Rouge men." It seemed a forlorn hope that these hard men could relent, but I had to place my hope in God.

I returned to the clinic wondering if the Lord would have worked a miracle before my arrival. I found that the situation was exactly the same, with the clinic chief still adamant about not letting An leave. However, he was getting fed up of us crying in front of his clinic, so finally he said: "I cannot make this decision, but you can go and ask the District Chief. If he agrees, then your brother can go."

Our hearts sank. The District Chief only came every month or so to visit our village. We looked at one another and knew that it was hopeless. How could we ever hope to find the District Chief in time to get to the railway station? Our grief increased and we began to cry even more loudly.

At that moment, I was reminded of the need to go to check on Somaly and Panita, who were guarding our belongings on the roadside about 20 metres away. They were probably hungry and I needed to find them something to eat. I went to where they were and found them sitting patiently.

As I was feeding Panita with some rice, I glanced round and there, before me, stood the District Chief. I could scarcely believe my eyes and I rushed towards him. Kneeling before him, with tears pouring down my face, I hardly dared to ask him for fear of being pushed aside.

The District Chief was astonished to see me in such a position and commanded: "Stand up. In this society you don't have to kneel and beg as in the old society. Just tell me, what is your request?"

I scrambled to my feet and blurted out: "All I want is permission to take my brother out of the clinic to come to Battambang with my family and myself."

"Has he been listed as one of your family?" the District Chief asked.

"Yes, of course," I replied.

"Then there is no problem. He has the right to go. Call the Village Chief so that I can check the list."

The Village Chief hurried over and confirmed that An was on our family list. My heart leapt as the District Chief granted permission for An to come with us. It was almost unbelievable how the power of God could operate in such a way.

As I rushed back to the clinic, I kept saying over and over again: "Thank you, Jesus. Thank you, Jesus." Seeing the clinic chief, I told him the news and he reluctantly agreed to release An. He had wanted to make trouble for us because of his dislike for An over the question of never working.

At the news, An jumped up and hobbled out of the clinic with the aid of a walking stick, saying that he didn't need any help. However, we could see that he was walking through the power of his own joy and not in his own strength.

A tremendous sense of relief washed through us all. God had performed a miracle to keep us all together. Gathering up our belongings, we set off once more into the unknown.

6   Terror on the Tracks

As we trudged out of Botrokar, bidding a less than fond farewell to our first experience of life under the Khmer Rouge, we were in a happy mood. We carried our various loads of personal belongings as if they were weightless. With one bag balanced on my head and another in my hand, I glanced round at the rest of the family. Only An and Panita, now two years old, didn't carry anything. Somaly, almost seven, carried a small bag on her head. She was growing up fast and had already proved to be an indispensable member of the family, carrying out tasks which many older children would have been unable to tackle. I often gave thanks to God for giving me two such lovely children to help me bear the separation from my husband.

An struggled along, leaning on his stick for support, and we set our pace so that he and Panita could easily keep up. We were already into the cool season and the sun was not too hot, which made our journey seem easier at the outset. We were not sure of the exact way, and so we simply tried to follow other groups of people. The strongest were already a long way ahead and only a few families with sick or old people straggled behind.

The road was hard with a gravel surface and wound between the paddy fields. It was difficult for all of us with no shoes, but especially so for the small children, although we were fortunate that it was fairly flat with no hills to climb. Trees overhung the road at intermittent intervals, but provided little shade. Within half an hour of leaving Botrokar, I could see that Panita was beginning to look tired. Each step was painful for her tiny feet, and yet I held back my words of sympathy. We were far behind the main group of villagers and I was fearful of missing the train. I had to hope that she could carry on for as long as possible and I didn't want to break her determination to keep up with the rest of us. However, eventually she could stand it no longer and she began to complain about her feet and her tiredness. An's face also became paler and paler, and sweat streamed down his swollen features. I felt sorry for him as I watched his trembling limbs. We stopped and rested. It was a welcome respite for us all, for we were all tired and the burden of our bags was beginning to tell.

We could only allow ourselves a few minutes before we were on our way again, but it was not long before we were forced to stop once more for a rest. The fear that we were the last people from the village and that we might lose our way urged us on. At last, it came to the point where poor Panita was crying and stumbling along at the same time and I realised that she would soon be unable to continue. All of us were already burdened with our bags but Mother, who had only one basket, offered to give Panita a piggyback ride. Mother was not well herself and she used a stick to help herself along. After a while, she put Panita down to walk a little by herself, but Panita soon began crying again. This time, An swung her up on his back and before long he passed her over to me. In this way, taking it in turns, we managed to continue until about 5 p.m. when we finally stopped to cook our rice.

We ate quickly both out of hunger and out of fear that the train would leave without us the next day. Then, gathering up our things, we continued walking. Even when it became dark, our footsteps didn't falter. Somehow we knew that we had to cover as much ground as possible if we wanted to reach the railway station by the next afternoon.

Gradually the blackness of the night increased until we could barely see more than a metre in front of our faces. Only Mother had the presence of mind, and the overriding desire not to lose anyone, to call out everyone's name about every ten minutes. In the dark, we had no clear idea of where we were going, but remembered that we had been told to follow the gravelled road.

All along the way, we heard the desperate shouts of parents who had lost sight of their children and the heart-rending screams of young children who had been separated from their parents. Their screams sent a chill through me and I stayed close to Somaly and Panita. It was largely due to Mother's insistence that we talk to each other that none of us became lost. We were all exhausted, stumbling along in the dark as if we were walking in our sleep, but Mother's shouts kept jerking us back to reality.

At around 9 p.m. we arrived at a village which had only one light showing. Our water was finished and our parched throats cried out for some. I went to one house in search of some water, and they directed me to the village pond. As I dipped our plastic containers into the water, I realised that it was stagnant and dirty, as it was only a few inches deep. However, we were desperate so I filled the containers and we drank deeply, filtering the leaves and insects with our teeth.

An hour later found us some way further, but too exhausted to continue. We lay down by the side of the road and slept on the ground. Mosquitos swarmed around us and bit every area of exposed skin, but we were too tired to take any notice. Waking up at about 4.30 a.m., we quickly cooked a meal, but ate only a small portion, saving the rest for our lunch later in the day. After a while, when we didn't see any other people from Botrokar on the road, we realised that we had got lost in the night. Coming upon another village, we asked the way to the railway station. Following their directions, we went in a straight line through the paddy fields and waded across a stream which came up to our waists. The crossing took us some time as we had to make several journeys to carry the children and our various baskets and bags. The fields were full of mud which sucked at our feet, but eventually the station came into sight and we arrived there at 5 p.m.

Our hearts sank as we noticed that all was quiet and the whole place was deserted. After all our effort and struggles, had we arrived too late and missed the train? We sank to the ground filled with despondency and not knowing what to do. In my despair, I prayed to God for His guidance in what seemed to be a hopeless situation.

A local villager passed nearby, and we called out to him: "Has the train left already?"

His answer gave us fresh hope: "No, the last train through here was two days ago."

Where had all the people gone then? We questioned the villager further:

"Did you see a large group of several hundred people?"

"Yes, they all went towards the temple." He pointed to the north and, as we stood on tiptoe on the raised railway tracks, we could just see the roof of the temple in the distance.

Even though we were tired and hungry, we were anxious to rejoin the villagers from Botrokar as soon as possible, in case they were about to embark on a train which we couldn't see. We hurried towards the temple, which lay about two kilometres away, and arrived at 6.30 p.m. as darkness was settling over the improvised campsite.

Talking to the other villagers from Botrokar, we found that many people had been sent from other villages to join us on the train. The Khmer Rouge had announced a delay of several days, and we were immediately sorry that we had hurried so much. As the darkness thickened, we found an open space and set up a plastic sheet for a roof and mosquito nets to keep away the insects which were already beginning to bite.

That night we slept well, and in the morning we reported to the Khmer Rouge leaders. We were given a tin of rice each and a little salt and sent out to find our own firewood for cooking. This proved very difficult as there were no trees in the vicinity, but only rice paddy fields. The lack of sanitation was an even greater problem, as there were no toilet facilities to cater for an influx of almost 2,000 people. In the daytime, people went into the nearest paddy field, which soon became well fertilised! However, during the night people relieved themselves close to the shelters, which made it difficult to walk around the campsite.

It was almost ten days before the Khmer Rouge finally announced that the train would arrive within one hour. Hastily throwing our meagre belongings into our bags, we began to hurry towards the station. Arriving there, we squatted down expecting the imminent arrival of the train. Our wait turned into an all-day vigil, which went on through the night. There was no room to lie down with so many people and so we dozed in a sitting position. It was very cold and the wind cut through our thin clothes. By morning, we were all damp from the night dew and we felt exhausted.

As the morning light grew and as we painfully exercised our frozen limbs, the train pulled into sight. It was a great relief and we all soon forgot our discomfort at the prospect of finally getting on our way. We were all divided into groups of 100 to 150 people and each group was assigned one carriage. Unfortunately, our group leader was slow and inefficient. While other groups quickly claimed the good carriages, we were left with an old restaurant carriage. It was smaller than the others and had no seats – only the fixed one-leg tables for eating. More than 100 of us were packed in like sardines and there was almost no room to sit on the floor. There were no overhead luggage racks in the restaurant carriage, so we put our possessions below and on top of one table. The whole family clustered round it, preserving 'our' space.

Two hours later, at 10 a.m., the train finally started on its way. The carriages were packed with people, and the number and weight of all the carriages was almost too much for the engine. It began very slowly and gradually built up speed. Even so, when we approached a slight gradient leading up to a bridge, the train was unable to get over it. We rolled backwards for another try, but were only successful at getting over the bridge at the fourth attempt after some people had been ordered off the train to walk over the bridge.

At the last station before Phnom Penh the train stopped. We were eager to get off and cook a meal, but the Khmer Rouge forbade us to leave the train. Instead, they came round distributing some food. We were amazed to have thrust into our hands some French bread and white sugar. It was a long time since we had seen anything like that and we ate greedily.

The Khmer Rouge also distributed one sardine per family. We gazed at the tiny fish in disbelief. There wasn't even enough for one bite each, so we broke it up into small pieces in a bowl and added some water. Then, dipping our bread into the paste, we ate without thinking of the future. Each adult with one loaf of bread and each child with half a loaf savoured the taste and for a time forgot the past. It was delicious and we ate it all. It was only later that we realised that this food was supposed to last for the whole train journey, and we had no idea how many hours or days it would take.

In the distance we could see the tall buildings of Phnom Penh rising majestically above the trees. We were very excited at seeing the capital again after almost a year and half-hoped that the Khmer Rouge would take us back into the city. However, when the train reached a side turning, we branched off towards Battambang. We were disappointed and sad to see Phnom Penh receding into the distance and we could only hope that our new destination would be better than Botrokar.

When we left that morning, we had imagined that the train would only take one day to reach Battambang, but it moved very slowly because it was so overloaded. During that first day, we didn't care because we had the thrill of seeing the open countryside rushing past and feeling the fresh breeze on our faces. The train stopped every two or three hours, but only for five to ten minutes. Because of the overcrowding, we took it in turns to sit and stand. Sometimes we talked between ourselves, speculating about our destination. At other times, we remained quiet, gazing out of the windows at the countryside, each silent with his or her own thoughts.

As night began to fall, we realised that we had a problem. We couldn't all sit down at the same time and we were becoming so tired that we needed to lie down, but there was no room. In addition, the combination of overcrowding, stuffiness and lack of food was beginning to have its effect as more and more people became sick. Our stomachs were not used to digesting bread, having been restricted to rice soup for so many months.

I managed to put Panita on to a corner of the table, where she curled up and went to sleep. Somaly huddled under the table and tried to sleep among the boxes and bags. There was nowhere for me to sleep and I had developed diarrhoea. I felt exhausted, but had to keep forcing my way through the crowded carriage to the toilet, which soon became blocked up until the stench was overpowering. Eventually, I could stand it no longer and I told my mother, who had managed to find a space to sit down, that I was going to search for a space in another carriage.

The other carriages were designed differently and had rows of seats on either side of an aisle which ran down the middle. The provision of overhead racks meant that most of the bags were out of the way. The seats were all crowded, but the aisle had been left free for people to pass up and down. It was just wide enough for my body and I lay down between the seats. I felt very sick and dozed fitfully, being constantly awakened by people going up and down the aisle. There was no light and so people stepped on me by mistake. Once a foot descended right on my face and my anguished yell startled its owner!

As dawn broke at 5 a.m. and light began to filter into the carriage, I remembered that Somaly and Panita were alone with Mother and I raised myself painfully to my feet. Forcing my bruised and aching muscles to function again, I rushed back to our carriage. As I entered, I heard a woman cry out in distress. Her baby had died in the night, and rivulets of tears streamed down her face. Others in the carriage, mindful of the rapid decomposition which would take place in the heat, had thrown the tiny body out of the window.

Somaly and Panita were still asleep, but Mother was awake, having slept little on a box of clothes. The faces of the rest of the family were haggard and drawn. I looked around at others in the carriage and their faces reflected my own – exhaustion, paleness and a look of sickness.

When the train stopped at about 10 a.m. we expected to be given food. We were sorely disappointed when the Khmer Rouge simply said that the bread had been intended to last for the whole journey. No one had expected the journey to last this long and had not brought any spare food with them. Those with small children, myself included, began to worry. Somaly and Panita looked hungry and the whole family could feel the hunger pains gnawing at their stomachs. We unpacked our bags and took out some spare, uncooked rice which we had carried with us. Other families copied our example and we also took out our cooking pot.

Having rice and a cooking pot was fine, but what about a stove, firewood, water and a place to cook? Our minds wrestled with what appeared to be insurmountable barriers. Children began to cry and it was a great relief to realise that the train was slowing down once more. Imagining that the Khmer Rouge had stopped to allow us time to cook, everyone rushed out of the train. The first thing we did was to search for three large stones. Placing these in a triangle, the cooking pot fitted nicely on top, and we had solved our stove problem. Other people simply dug a hole in the ground and placed the pot on top of it. Our next step was to find some firewood. This was easier said than done because those who weren't fast enought in snatching up odd sticks lying close to the railway line had to go further afield, thus wasting precious time. I had just placed our cooking pot on the three stones and was joining the others in searching for wood when, with only a blast on its whistle as a warning, the train began to move again. There was instant confusion up and down the tracks as panic set in. I snatched up the pot with rice in, screaming at Da and Srey Vy to grab wood so that we could be ready for the next stop. Peauv came running up with the empty water container, having been unable to find any water, and together we ran towards the train doors. It was absolute chaos as we all tried to climb in at the same time. I felt sorry for those who had managed to half-boil their rice as they struggled to carry their hot cooking pots back into the train.

The train started slowly as usual and finally everyone managed to get in after running alongside. I was thankful that we had left Mother, Somaly, Panita and An, who was still sick and weak, on the train. Otherwise, it would have been almost impossible to get them all on board.

As we settled down again and began to get our breath back, we discussed our strategy for cooking the rice at the next stop. Since Da and Srey Vy had managed to save a little wood at the previous stop, we decided that our first step must be to search for three stones. Then, having lit the fire, we would have to risk using our reserve supply of drinking water so that the rice could begin cooking immediately, while Peauv went off to search for more water.

After two hours the train began to slow down once more, and we headed for the door. This time everything went according to plan and we managed to cook our rice. Peauv was also able to find water to replenish our drinking supply. We carried the rice in the pot back on to the train. Others had taken longer and had to run for the train again as it moved away. We added salt to the rice and gathered round the pot to eat the rice. Somaly and Panita were especially hungry, and I made sure that they had enough to eat.

Later on, in the early afternoon, while the train was stopped, several people carried the corpse of an old man down from the train and buried him in a shallow grave by the railway tracks. I heard that others had died during the night and had been thrown out of the windows while the train was still moving.

The length of the stops was unpredictable and the Khmer Rouge gave no advance warning of the train's departure. A stop might last for as long as 20 minutes or it might be as short as five minutes, depending on the whim of the Khmer Rouge. At one stop, Da took Somaly off to go to the toilet. They went quite far off as there was no shelter close to the train. It seemed that they had no sooner disappeared from view than the train gave a blast on its whistle. I was at the window scanning the faces of the people rushing back to the train, but there was no sign of either Somaly or Da. As the train started to move, my heart began to hammer and I faced the dreadful possibility of losing Somaly and Da. The train gathered speed and I saw Da rush

out of the forest. Of Somaly, there was no sign and my
heart sank.

I screamed: "Where is Somaly? Come on, come on!" Da
stopped and waited for Somaly, who then came into view.
With the train pulling past them, I felt a shock of horror as
I contemplated my alternatives. Should I jump down and
stay with Somaly, leaving Panita with Mother, or should
I stay on board the train with Panita and abandon Somaly
and Da in the middle of the forest?

My mind refused to consider either possibility and I
rushed to the door, exhorting them to run faster, faster . . .
The train was overloaded and it took time to get up speed.
Little by little, Da and Somaly came level with our carriage
door. Somaly's lips were almost blue with fright and the
effort of running alongside the moving train. Da scrambled
up the steps and I leaned down and grabbed Somaly's hand.
Her feet left the ground and, as her weight pulled me
outwards, her shins bumped briefly on the ground. Then,
anchoring myself to the door with my other hand, I hauled
her through the doorway. We clung to each other shaking
with weariness and relief. The train had stopped in a very
remote area and Somaly would surely have died if she had
been left behind.

Chaos reigned again in mid-afternoon, as everyone tried
to cook their evening meal. We tried to cook our rice in
one stop, but again shortage of time forced us to complete
the cooking at the next stop. This time I made sure that
none of the family strayed out of sight of the train.

As the afternoon wore on, we entered Battambang Province. At fairly regular intervals we passed small encampments alongside the railway tracks. We realised that other
groups had been transferred before us and had been dropped
off at different spots to hack new paddy fields out of
the jungle. Some encampments were deserted with plastic
sheets flapping in the wind and a look and smell of death.
In other encampments, a few people came out to stand and

stare dully at the train as we chugged past. We began to fear for our own future and wondered if we would share a similar fate, abandoned in the forest without supplies.

Some time later, the train reached Battambang City, which was the largest city in western Cambodia and used to have a large market. It was a centre of some considerable wealth, being in the middle of a rich agricultural belt. We half hoped that we might be asked to settle there, but the train didn't stop. It carried on until it finally came to a halt at the town of Sisophon, one of the large district towns. We were all told to get out, an order with which we gladly complied. A feeling of relaxation settled over us, as we were at last able to walk around without having to worry about the train leaving without us. We took our bags out of the train and settled down to wait for new orders. After a while a loudspeaker announcement told us to sort ourselves out into groups of ten families and appoint group leaders. The leader had to make a list of names and then go to collect rice for his group. We soon found ourselves in a group of families and selected a leader. We located a scrap of paper and wrote down all our names. As is the Khmer custom, I was using my husband's name and simply called myself Mrs Lach Virak Phong.

Our group leader went off with the list of names to collect the rice. He presented the list to the Khmer Rouge chief, so that the correct quantity of rice could be measured out. Scanning the list, the Khmer Rouge chief spotted the name of Lach Virak Phong and asked, "Where is Virak Phong?"

Our group leader replied: "No, he's not here. It's only his wife." A gleam of interest showed in the Khmer Rouge man's eyes and he ordered: "Send her to see me, because her husband is a friend of mine."

Our group leader returned to us with the rice. As he began to distribute it to each family, he told me of the exchange with the Khmer Rouge chief and advised me to go and see him. I was on the point of going, hoping to receive an extra ration of rice from this 'friend' of my husband's, when Somaly began to cry complaining of a stomach ache. I turned to comfort her, telling myself that I would go to see the Khmer Rouge chief later. As I became involved with preparations to leave the station and find a place to stay, I was too busy and never found enough time to go and see him.

Afterwards I heard that the Khmer Rouge had arrested several people whose names they had recognised on the lists. These people were never heard of again and it was widely rumoured that they had been taken away and killed. I realised that the continued use of my husband's name could lead us all into danger, so from then on I reverted to being known by my maiden name of Hong Var. I gave thanks to God for using Somaly's stomach ache to prevent me from going to almost certain death.

We cooked our rice and then found a deserted house near the station to sleep in. All the other people easily found accommodation in empty houses as the whole population of Sisophon had been forced out of the town months previously.

At 6 a.m. in the morning, loudspeakers announced that we would all shortly be leaving in a convoy of tractors and trailers. We hurried to cook our rice and to eat breakfast. By 7 a.m. the convoy had arrived. Each trailer held a group of ten families and we were called out to be loaded on to them. The convoy set off and we soon discovered that our driver had hardly ever driven before. He weaved from side to side of the road, and I wondered if I had escaped death from the Khmer Rouge only to be killed by this mad driver.

My worst fears were realised as the tractor careered off the road, down the embankment and into the small canal alongside. The trailer bounced wildly after the tractor, almost overturning, while everyone screamed in fear. Two men were thrown off the trailer. One man's arm was trapped in the frame, but another was pinned underneath the trailer with his head barely above water. Several of the children were bruised and we were all shaking with fright. It took us until 6 p.m. to free the men and to get the tractor and trailer out of the canal with the help of another tractor.

It was 9 p.m. before we finally arrived at the place for our overnight stop. We were in the middle of the Cambodian 'winter' and the strong wind made us extremely cold, causing us to shiver constantly. We quickly made a shelter from four poles, two of them being An's and Mother's walking sticks, and covered them with a plastic sheet. It was too windy to get a fire going and anyway it was so dark that it would have been impossible to find any wood. We were too tired to cook and simply lay down and tried to sleep. Somaly and Panita shivered with the cold and we all huddled together. The long day and their tiredness made them cry a little, but they eventually dropped off to sleep.

In the early morning as dawn broke, I got up to search for firewood and cooked our breakfast of rice. The Khmer Rouge announced that the journey would continue by ox-cart. Along with our bags, Mother and Panita were allowed to sit on the ox-cart. Somaly trotted alongside, struggling to keep up.

In this way we travelled for about ten kilometres before arriving at our new home – a village called Trar Paing Thmar.

7 The Fatal Salute

Trar Paing Thmar, a district of Battambang Province, seemed to be the same size as Botrokar, but whereas Botrokar had a somewhat modern atmosphere, this village had a typical rural look to it and had a rather desolate air. We were sent to share a small house with another family, who were the original owners. However, the Khmer Rouge considered all houses to be the property of the Angkar after the revolution. All the newcomers were split up among the village's original inhabitants and no one was given the choice of where they were put or with whom they stayed.

The house to which we were allocated contained a couple with two children. Their oldest was a 16-year-old girl and the youngest was an 18-month-old baby boy. The house itself was fairly simple. It was largely of wood construction with a roof fabricated from corrugated tin sheets. It was built on stilts, which allowed the passage of air underneath and was very appropriate for a hot country. At the top of the steps were two doors. The one on the right led off to a small kitchen and the one straight ahead led to the main part of the house. The house itself was almost entirely bare. Towards the back, at the right, was a small area which had been partitioned off into a room. The family who were already living there kept all their belongings inside that room and their daughter slept there. The couple, who were around 40 years old, slept with the baby just outside the bedroom. The whole house was about eight metres square. That night our entire family slept in a long line down the left-hand side of the house. It was a squash but being able to lie down after our cramped train journey made it seem not too bad.

The next morning we were awakened early and sent off to work in the fields. The temperature was quite low and we shivered with the cold as we were wading through water to get to our assigned area of work. Before leaving the village, we had all been issued with scythes to cut the long rice stalks which were laden with rice grains. We took a handful of stalks, swung our scythes and then laid the cut stems down behind us. When there were enough stems, they were tied up into large bundles and collected later into a large pile.

The village of Trar Paing Thmar contained no hard-core Khmer Rouge and the village leaders had been appointed by the Khmer Rouge from among the original inhabitants. The leaders proved to be quite pleasant and there was not the same atmosphere of fear as we had experienced in Botrokar. In fact, there was very little to compare our present lives with our former existence. Life was much easier and we worked happily. We were given decent food and, because it was harvest time, there was more than enough rice to eat. We were allowed to cook our own rice as a family in the village. However, the lunch-time food was prepared by the commune in a central place and then dispensed only to the villagers who worked in the fields. Those who did not work received only salt. Every day we were given either meat or fish which they had cooked with vegetables, making it into a different kind of soup each day. The food nourished our bodies and enabled us to put more energy into our work.

Our day started at around 4.30 a.m., when we arose to cook rice which we would carry with us to the fields to eat later. We left the village between 5 and 5.30 a.m. while Mother stayed behind to take care of Panita. Somaly had now started to work with other children, who were ordered to do light tasks around the village such as weeding the gardens, collecting animal dung and disposing of rubbish. The rest of us had to walk almost five kilometres to get to the rice fields. Arriving there at about 6 a.m., we immediately began work and continued until about 11 a.m., when we stopped to eat lunch. This was our first meal of the day and five hours of work gave us ravenous appetites. We had all brought our own rice and the leaders distributed a vegetable and fish soup which had been brought from the village by ox-cart. We all sat down in small groups waiting to receive the hand-out and then we were allowed to sit and eat happily together for an hour. At midday we went back to work in the fields and continued until 5 p.m.

It was often 6 p.m. or later before we arrived back at the village. After washing ourselves, cooking and eating our evening meal, which consisted of only rice and salt, we were allowed to rest for a short while. Those with gold were able to secretly barter it for dried or pickled fish. The day was not yet over, even though sometimes our bodies craved sleep. The village leader came round at around 8 to 8.30 p.m. to order us to begin work again. This time we didn't have to walk very far, as the work consisted of threshing the rice which had been cut and which had been gathered up and placed in ox-carts for transporting to the village earlier in the day. In the middle of the village a special area had been prepared for the threshing. An area of ground 30 metres by 40 metres had been cleared, levelled and smoothed over with wet mud and left to dry. Now a hard clean surface, it was ready for the threshing.

In western countries, grain harvesting is carried out by combine harvesters which perform several jobs at the same time. Cutting, threshing and cleaning of the grain is done mechanically. However, what little machinery had existed before had been left to rust in the sheds and the fields. There was virtually no fuel in the country to run the machinery and, anyway, the Khmer Rouge distrusted technology of any sort, believing it to have a corrupting influence. They wanted everything done in a primitive way and now all these tasks had to be carried out manually. The men and women of the village stood in a long line in front of a sloping board. Behind them was the large pile of rice stalks that had been cut during the day. Grasping a bundle of rice stems using two short wooden sticks held in both hands, they hit the stems several times against the board so that the rice grains were shaken off and slid down the board on to the ground. Others gathered the rice, which was all mixed up with husks and dust, into small trays. Standing on a small wooden platform, they poured the rice into other trays on the ground so that the breeze would blow away the dust and chaff, gradually cleaning the rice. Then the rice grains were put aside to dry for one or two days before it was ready to be carried away to the barn for storage. During the evening, a small amount of sweet mung bean porridge was distributed to everyone. Work finally finished at about 11 p.m., when we fell exhausted into our 'beds'.

Bed for us consisted of a mat unrolled on to the wooden floor. I had a piece of material which I was able to use as a blanket and I covered Somaly and Panita with it as well. The nights were cold, so the owner of the house put a piece of tin sheeting on several bricks in the middle of the floor. Piling earth around the outside, he lit a fire in the middle. This helped to take the chill out of the nights and kept us reasonably warm until the weather warmed up at the end of January 1976.

Behind our house grew one of several sugar palm trees, and every morning a man would come to climb the tree. He collected the sweet juice which would later be made into palm sugar. It was sweet and people craved it after a diet which consisted of little more than rice. The value of palm sugar was very high and it was thought of as liquid gold. My mother said to me one night: "If we could only make friends with the man who climbs the palm tree, maybe I would have the chance to taste palm juice again before I die." It seemed a forlorn hope at the time.

After the harvest season was over, our work was no longer so intense. Although still hard, we worked more reasonable hours and found a little time to relax. With little agricultural work to do, we were ordered to dig a small canal around the village. We were divided into groups and each group was given a different section to construct. As a reward for our hard work, the Khmer Rouge decided to give a small piece of palm sugar to each person. The leader of the palm sugar manufacturing plant and his assistant were ordered to take it around for distribution. When they reached our group and began the distribution, they became trapped into conversation. There were many talkative girls and we each tried to wheedle more sugar out of the two men. The leader and I got into conversation and he asked me where I lived in the village. As we talked, we realised that it was he who came each morning to climb the palm tree behind our house. A few days later, I managed to see him again and asked him secretly if it would be possible to have a cup of the juice for my mother. It was a dangerous move on my part because the Khmer Rouge hated anyone who tried to improve their diet of rice. At first he was reluctant because of the danger, but he eventually agreed as long as I told no one else. From then on, he left a cup of juice behind our house each morning and we shared it out among ourselves. Often, in the evenings, the leader and his assistant came to visit us in our home and we spent many hours talking to them about the new life under the Khmer Rouge. This took the form of some positive input on our part as we tried to praise the policy of the Angkar as much as possible. This was necessary so that word of our 'loyalty' would filter back to the Khmer Rouge leaders.

After two months, a rumour spread in the village that the Khmer Rouge were looking for educated persons and previous military personnel to send to Phnom Srok, the district town, for 're-education'. They tried to convince everyone that they wanted such people to help them rebuild the system of government under the Angkar. Some of the old civil servants declared themselves openly but those who had been soldiers under the Lon Nol regime were afraid and concealed their identity. Two or three times a week for the next two weeks, the village chief and the group leaders came round all the houses asking people about their life under the Lon Nol regime. An, my brother, told them that he was a mechanic and that he had serviced old vehicles in one of the suburbs of Phnom Penh. He had some knowledge of the inner workings of vehicles and so he hoped to be able to convince the Khmer Rouge if he was ever put to the test. I told them honestly that I had been a teacher before, although I refrained from mentioning that I had taught English and also spoke French. Others in the family were too young to have had a profession under the previous regime, except for Lay, who told them that he was a farmer from the countryside.

For a while we hoped that we would escape further scrutiny and that our stories had satisfied the Khmer Rouge. Then, disaster struck. One of the recent new arrivals to the village was an ex-soldier who had been a member of An's unit, when he had been a second-lieutenant. Upon meeting An unexpectedly one day in the middle of the village, he suddenly brought his heels together and stood to attention in front of An. It was an instinctive reaction on the part of the soldier, brought about through many years of training to show respect to a senior officer. However, in this context it was catastrophic. I was with An at the time and I caught my breath in horror. An, himself, looked quickly away. As the full realisation of what he had done dawned on the soldier, a look of guilt transformed his face from respect to terror. He shuffled off down a little side street, but his action had not gone unnoticed. Our group leader had seen it all and, in a bid to curry favour with the Khmer Rouge, went straight to report the incident.

Not long afterwards, the village chief distributed a list of names which gave details of all the people whom the Angkar had decided were needed in Phnom Srok. Not all the people who had confessed to being former civil servants were on the list. However, all ex-soldiers of the Lon Nol regime were listed. An's name was there, and we all felt a terrible sense of impending loss when we saw his name. Amazingly, my name was not there. Perhaps, they had kept me because I had worked hard (which meant, in their minds, that I fully supported the Angkar) or maybe they had decided that I should stay to help take care of the rest of the family. It was difficult to know how the Khmer Rouge thought because other teachers' names were on the list.

Those who were on the list were told to stay in the village and wait for trucks to come and take them away. The rest of us were sent out to work in the fields. Several trucks came each day to take people away, and we never knew if we would find An there at the end of the day or not. We never really had a chance to say a proper goodbye to him. We simply came back one day and he was gone. Altogether over 1,000 people were taken.

We continued working and waited desperately for some news. For a month there was nothing. Inexplicably, a woman who had been taken away to Phnom Srok was allowed to come back to Trar Paing Thmar. She had not stayed very long in Phnom Srok and so could not give us much information about what was happening there. However, she was able to tell us about the truck journey. I questioned her closely, and she told me that during the journey one man had jumped out of the back of one truck and had tried to run away into the forest. All the trucks had halted and, while a few Khmer Rouge had stayed to guard the trucks, most of the others, armed with their

AK47s, had given chase to the fugitive. He wasn't able to get far and long before he had reached the concealment of the forest he had been gunned down from behind in full view of everyone in the trucks. It had been a sobering message to any other would-be escapers and no one else had tried.

Almost fearfully, I asked the woman to describe the man who had run away. She said that he had a moustache and was wearing a white sweater and a pair of blue jeans. A terrible pain constricted my heart as I realised that she was describing An. That was what he had been wearing on the day we had last seen him. I could hardly bring myself to believe it. Surely he was not dead. It was a nightmare. Maybe the woman's description was wrong or perhaps someone else had been wearing the same type of clothing. We would certainly hear from him soon. Little by little, my mind tried to discount what I had heard and I kept a little hope that he might yet be alive. Even though I could not bring myself to believe that An was dead, his absence from the family was a loss to me. I had relied so much on him for strength and help in leading our small group. I felt truly bereft without him. I said nothing to my mother, who would have been absolutely desolate to know that her eldest son was dead. However, someone else told my mother that she had seen An in Reneam, a place where tons and tons of salted and smoked fish were produced for export. She said that An was fine, except that he suffered from malaria from time to time. This gave my mother hope that she would one day see him again. I held out no hope for him, believing that he was dead.

It was some time later that more stories began to filter back to us of what had taken place in Phnom Srok. There was no way that we could verify them, but they sounded very much like the way that the Khmer Rouge would have behaved in their efforts to weed out those people who were tied to the former regime. It seemed that several days after the more than 1,000 people had arrived in Phnom Srok, the Khmer Rouge had prepared a banquet in a large hall and had then invited everyone to dinner. As the people arrived in the hall, they found that the tables had been laid in three different ways. One group of tables had white tablecloths, silver cutlery, napkins, crystal glasses and beautiful china. The second set of tables had no tablecloths, but were set out with ordinary plates, cutlery and spoons. The third group of tables had tin plates or chipped ceramic plates, metal spoons and plastic mugs. Once everyone was inside the hall, the Khmer Rouge leader stood up to make a speech. First, he welcomed everyone. Then, in a sweet voice, he thanked people for being willing to help in the enormous task of rebuilding the country. He apologised that there was not enough good cutlery and crockery to go around, but said that there were enough places for all and enough food so no one needed to worry. Finally, he asked everyone to find a seat and sit down.

It is easy with hindsight to understand the Khmer Rouge motives and to see how they were trying to trick people. However, those people, who had a genuine desire to help in the reconstruction of their country and who were lured into a false sense of security by the sweetness of the welcome afforded them, were easily taken in. The upper class Cambodians, who were used to city life and to high standards of living, automatically graduated towards the tables with the tablecloths and crystal glasses. Those who had lived in the cities, but who were ordinary people, headed towards the second set of tables which were laid out in the manner to which they had been accustomed. Finally, the working-class people instinctively sat down around the tables with tin plates and metal spoons. This, after all, was what they had more or less been used to eating with all their lives.

The same food was served to all the people regardless of which table they were at. At the end of the meal, the Khmer Rouge announced that the people sitting around the tables with cloths should stay behind as they had something to say to these 'important' people. Everyone else left the hall and then the people who still thought along the lines of the old society were taken away, never to be heard from again.

The people who survived this dinner were eventually able to send letters to their relatives in Trar Paing Thmar. Little by little, news filtered in of those who were still known to be alive. I finally had come to accept that even if it had not been An who had been shot trying to escape from the truck, he must be dead as we had heard nothing from him.

Although Mother didn't know of the story about someone jumping out of the truck and being killed, she became desolate since there was no news of An, while other people had been able to send news to their families. The disappearance of An was a terrible blow to her. Her eyesight, already weak and failing due to lack of medical care, worsened quickly, until she could only tell light from darkness. Little Panita, now two and a half, became her guide, sitting near her, guiding her hand to the rice plate, bringing her water, leading her to the toilet . . . but Mother had to ask many questions before she could trust such a young guide.

Life in the village continued and we were allowed no time to indulge in family grief. The time for night work was mostly over except for the occasional moon-lit night when we were ordered out to do odd jobs such as digging ditches or levelling nearby roads. The evenings became our own except for the once or twice-weekly 're-education' meetings, when we were taught about the Angkar revolution and told what we should do to support the movement. We had been hearing the same thing for more than a year now.

In May, the relative tranquillity was disturbed as I developed diarrhoea while staying at a site five kilometres away from the village where we were digging a canal. At first, I thought it was just a normal stomach upset from which everyone in the village suffered from time to time due to contaminated water sources. However, this time the diarrhoea continued for days and my stools deteriorated into mainly blood and mucus. I lost my appetite and became so weak that I could no longer climb up and down the stairs outside the house. Mother quickly took charge. She sent the others out to the neighbours' houses to look for old planks of wood. With the help of others, she arranged these on bricks underneath the house. I was carefully led downstairs and was helped to lie down on the planks. The bricks allowed the air to circulate underneath the planks and kept me cool.

It seemed that I was suffering from a form of amoebic dysentery which was slowly destroying me. Mother stayed with me all the time, wiping my face with a damp cloth and trying to comfort me. Lay and Sokhon had been sent away to work in another village, while Peauv and Da had been sent to work in the Youth Brigade outside of our village. Apart from Mother, only Srey Vy, Somaly and Panita were left. Without Mother's nursing, I would have died and I came to appreciate the strong hands that cared for me and the unseeing eyes that gazed lovingly at me.

It was not long before I was so weak that I did not even have the strength to get up and crawl to the nearest bush to relieve myself. Mother solved the problem by placing the planks on which I lay slightly apart so that I could relieve myself at any time on the ground below. Twice a day, with the help of Somaly and Panita, Mother shovelled out the excrement from underneath the planks and Somaly carried it away and buried it. Then Somaly brought ashes from the fire to put under the planks to try and eliminate the smell.

The Khmer Rouge still provided food for Mother and the children, who tried to coax me into eating a small amount at each meal, but I had no appetite and just lay there listlessly. I could feel myself becoming thinner and thinner and I knew that I had lost a tremendous amount of weight. There was no modern medicine in the village and no doctors. Mother, led by Somaly or Panita, went round the houses in the village, begging people to give her some traditional medicine so that she could treat my dysentery. Over a period of time, she was able to procure roots and herbs which she brought back to the house to cook up. One of the vital ingredients which was missing for this brew was sugar. She solved that problem by approaching the leader of the palm sugar factory. He gave some to her and she began to cook it all together. When it was finished, she brought a glass of the foul smelling mixture over to me to drink. I could hardly stand the smell, but I was so sick that I was willing to try anything to get better. I had never tasted anything so bitter in my life, but I forced myself to drink it.

Other villagers, with whom I had established superficial relationships, came up with recipes which they said were sure to cure my illness. These included a steamed cake made from yeast, palm sugar and rice flour. I didn't feel like eating, but the knowledge that cake in any form was extremely rare made me swallow it. Another recipe consisted of ripe tamarind liberally sprinkled with salt. Something amongst all these different remedies must have worked because I eventually got better and my stools returned to normal. However, the illness had left its mark on me. My skin was very pale and I felt like a skeleton with skin stretched over it. My eyes were sunk deep into my face. My husband would never have recognised me if he had seen me then. The village chief came round to see me several times a week. This was not out of pity. Rather, he wanted to check when I would be strong enough to return to work. The Khmer Rouge leaders didn't like anyone who didn't pull their weight.

I had been ill for about a month and I had still not returned to work by June when the village chief went round the village telling different families that they were required to move to a new village in three days' time. By the end of the third evening, I began to feel a sense of relief that our names had not been called. However, at 9 p.m. that night, when most people were already asleep, the village chief came to our house. He apologised for coming so late and said that he had not intended that I should leave the village. However, a number of villagers who were due to leave had especially requested that I go also. I did not know why. Any friendships that I had with other villagers lacked depth. Everyone was afraid to trust another person in case he or she turned out to be a Khmer Rouge informer. Even so, I got on fairly well with most people and perhaps some of them had asked for me to go. On the other hand, perhaps someone who disliked me wanted me to leave since no one knew what awaited us at the other end of the road.

Lay and Sokhon were working away from the village, but returned that evening to collect more supplies for the Khmer Rouge. Lay and Sokhon were considered as one family unit, and the rest of us were considered as another. In order to stay together, we asked if Lay and Sokhon could also come, and the village chief agreed. He also sent for Da and Peauv, so that they could arrive very early the following morning.

That night, Mother did all the packing, helped by Somaly and Srey Vy. In the morning, as dawn broke, I hobbled out to the main road with the help of a stick and everyone followed behind. We waited there to be collected by a small convoy of ox-carts, one of which had been promised to each family for the journey. When the ox-carts finally came into view, we selected one and piled our belongings inside. Mother, Panita and I climbed on as well, while the others walked alongside. Only later on, as Somaly tired, did we manage to persuade the ox-cart driver to let Somaly clamber on the cart with us.

The rainy season had already begun and it rained in

torrents all day. Although we had a plastic sheet to cover us and our belongings on the cart, the rain worked its way insidiously underneath and we soon became soaked through just like those who walked alongside. The ox-cart drivers stopped for us to cook rice at midday. However, there was nothing we could do. There was no dry firewood and we couldn't cook in the middle of the rain. We stayed hungry and continued on our way.

At some point in the morning we turned off the main road on to a little track which was heavily overgrown. It was barely more than a pathway and the ox-carts bumped up and down. On top of the cart, I was thrown from side to side. In my weakened condition, I soon became exhausted and felt as if I were going to die under the hammer blows of the sides of the cart as I was repeatedly struck against them.

We continued deeper into the forest and as the afternoon wore on, the sun began to fall below the horizon. Night came quickly, the darkness being hastened by the canopy of tree branches above. Some of the smaller wild animals, disturbed by our passing, crashed through the undergrowth and disappeared. At around 8 p.m. we arrived at a village. The sight of it was like food to a starving man. At last we would be able to rest. However, our hopes were dashed when the Khmer Rouge ordered only a few families to stay there. The rest of us continued into the night. Two more villages were passed and each time several more families peeled off to begin a new life there. Our family was among the few that were ordered to keep on going. The sound of the ox-carts by now was greatly reduced.

Through the night a small light glimmered between the trees not very far away. It seemed to take for ever to arrive, but when we got there we found it was the only light in the whole village. It was set in the little hut that was used as a clinic to treat sick people with traditional medicine. As we waited, the rain petered out to a few small splashing drops. It took about half an hour before the ox-carts were allowed to drop families off at different houses in the village. Meanwhile, I lay curled up in the cart, shivering with the cold. I had no strength to talk, let alone to sit up. Along the way, my mother had kept talking to me and shaking me by the shoulder. It was annoying and I kept wishing that she would stop. Since I wasn't strong enough even to talk, I had to endure it. It was only later that I realised that my mother, seeing me almost motionless, was afraid that I was about to die and she had been trying to keep me awake.

Eventually, the village chief finished allocating all the newcomers to different houses and we were led off to the one that had been assigned to us. It was a relief to get out of the cart. I staggered up the house steps with someone's help and collapsed on the floor. The owner was very kind and rushed to the kitchen to cook up some hot rice porridge for us to eat together with some salted preserved fish. It wasn't much, but after the misery of the day, it seemed as if we were sitting inside a nice warm restaurant eating steak.

We had arrived in Svay Sar, which was to be our home for the next 16 months.

8   The Horror of the Leeches

Svay Sar seemed to be in the middle of the forest close to the foot of two mountains. At night we could hear the cries of wild pigs, wolves and tigers. The trees pressed around the village, hemming us in. Each field seemed to have been hacked from the jungle, which now gave the appearance of trying to reclaim its territory. The people of the village were known as 'jungle' people. This savage-sounding term did not do justice to them for, contrary to our expectations, they were a good-hearted people and we all felt relieved. The Khmer Rouge leaders were able to see from my appearance that I was recovering from a serious sickness and did not ask me to go out immediately to work. They said that I could rest until I had recovered my strength, so I was able to stay at home for about two weeks. Everyone else in the family went out to work as before.

Even Mother, who was now blind, was forced to work. Her unseeing eyes were wide open all the time and the Khmer Rouge would not believe that she was blind. They sent her out to the fields to pick the leaves from the mulberry bushes, which would later be fed to the silk worms. Poor Mother could only pick by feeling the leaves and so, as she shuffled down the rows, she picked whatever leaves she was able to touch. Not only mulberry leaves went into her bag, but also leaves from poisonous climbing plants which were intertwined with the mulberry bushes. When the supervisor came to check on her work, she was furious and began shouting at Mother, thinking that she was trying to sabotage the small weaving industry in the village. Mother told her again that she was blind and the supervisor swung her hand at Mother's eyes. Mother didn't blink and the supervisor realised that she had been telling the truth. Still, she was not allowed to stay at home. Instead, they sent her to look after the small babies who were left lying in hammocks for most of the day while the mothers went out to work nearby. Her job was to rock the hammocks and to call the mothers whenever she could not manage on her own.

Life seemed pleasant at first. However, what seemed like a balmy existence quickly turned to fear when I saw what happened to one other lady who was always sick like me. She was taken away by the Khmer Rouge and did not return. I could not believe that they would actually have killed her for being sick, but the other villagers said that the Angkar had disposed of her because she was lazy and they wanted to make an example of her to the whole village. Laziness was a crime which was not tolerated in the new society.

In the village was one man who had the skills and techniques of a traditional doctor. Such men were not trained in modern medicine, but they had an intimate knowledge of herbs and wild roots which grew in the forest. The combination of these was often sufficient to cure some of the maladies common to the people who lived in the middle of the jungle. This traditional doctor took a liking to me and brought me food as well as some traditional medicine. I gradually began to recover my strength until I was strong enough to start work again.

My fear of the Khmer Rouge subsided as I went out to work with a group of mothers with small babies. They allowed me to work with that group because I still looked very weak and thin. Normally, mothers with children of the same age as mine were sent to work in distant fields. However, those with small babies were allowed to work close to the village so that they could be near their children in case of need. There were several cucumber fields near the village to which I was assigned. As I weeded and picked the cucumbers, I began to eat them at the same time. This was a dangerous action on my part as it was strictly forbidden by the Khmer Rouge. However, it filled my stomach and enabled me to gain strength. I ate secretly as I crouched over the plants and in one day I often ate as many as 10 to 20 small young cucumbers. The others in the fields, both the new arrivals and the original inhabitants, did the same, but no one reported it since we were all hungry. I was very fortunate to be allowed to stay and work in the cucumber field, while others slaved away planting rice.

When we first arrived at the village, we were assigned to stay with another family. Before long, we were ordered to construct our own house. 'House' is too grand a word to describe the dwelling which we were allowed to build for ourselves. The small hut which we constructed was about three metres square. The Khmer Rouge gave us some thatch for the roof, but we had to find all the other materials ourselves. We took it in turns to go out into the forest to look for the necessary material. We cut down small trees for the corner posts and made logs to support the floor. Branches formed the rafters, which held the grass thatch as the roof. Nails were non-existent, so Lay and Peauv clambered up the big trees in the forest and cut down the creepers which trailed down. We cut them up into smaller strips, notched the wood, and then tied the pieces of wood together to make the house firm. Finally we laid thin strips of bamboo to make a floor to sleep on. Having made it ourselves, we felt a certain sense of pride at being able to construct our own home.

Compared with the tiny quantities of food which we had been allowed in the previous village, the amounts in Svay Sar seemed quite generous. Together with the rice, there was almost always some fish and vegetables. We were also permitted to go and fish in the nearby ponds and streams. It provided a valuable source of extra protein for us. During the rainy season, we were able to go into the forest and find all sorts of wild vegetables, bamboo shoots and onion-like roots. From time to time, some of the villagers went off to hunt in the forest. They came back with wild boar, deer and wildfowl, which was then cooked and shared out among all the villagers. Life could almost have been idyllic, if there had not been the ever-present fear of being killed for saying the wrong thing.

When the Khmer Rouge considered that I was strong enough, I was sent to work with a group of young women far from the village. We were given a variety of jobs which varied with the season and all of which involved hard physical labour. Some days we were put to work clearing the forest so that more land could be opened up for cultivation. Other days we dug irrigation canals or built small dams. There didn't seem to be much logic about where canals or dams were sited. It almost seemed as if the Khmer Rouge wanted to give us work for the sake of work without thinking through the usefulness of what we were doing.

One afternoon, while working under the burning sun, I began to feel light-headed and my body became colder and colder until I could hardly stand. I lay down on the ground curling up into a ball in an effort to keep warm. The Khmer Rouge came running over to check what was going on and concluded that I was having an attack of malaria. I was sent home where I alternated from hot to cold, from running a high temperature and sweating to shivering with cold. I felt totally exhausted. The traditional medicine doctor came from time to time to give me herbal medicine, which made me vomit continuously until my whole body felt like jelly. The attack was so severe that it took almost a month for me to recover sufficiently to return to the fields.

It was not long before harvest time came round. The rice

stems waved in the fields as the breeze blew and seemed to be beckoning us to work. Each of the 'new' people was assigned a one-metre width to harvest. We all started in a long line and gradually moved forwards. I had not fully recovered from the attack of malaria and the strain of constantly bending over soon took its toll. During the first day under the hot sun I fainted. Apparently, no one paid any attention to me because they thought I was pretending. I lay there unconscious while the other people moved forward. When I came to my senses, I got up and began work again. My head was aching and my body was trembling. It seems silly, but I did not dare to go to the side of the field and lie down. During the next three days, it seemed that I spent more time unconscious on the ground after fainting than I did actually standing up and harvesting rice. The fields were a long way from the village and when the time came to go home in the evening, I was always the last to arrive at the village as I dragged my weary body home. Though the other villagers had thought at first that I was pretending, they could see that I was becoming paler and paler. During the short time allotted for lunch in the middle of the day, I didn't have enough strength to crawl to the lunch area. I think that was what finally convinced them that I was sick. I was allowed to return to the village, where I was assigned to work in the cucumber field again. The less strenuous work and the opportunity to eat the cucumbers surreptitiously again enabled me gradually to rebuild my strength.

During this time, Somaly had been sent to work with a junior group. The children also harvested rice – schooling and education was considered unnecessary. Learning in any form, except about the Angkar and the revolution, was not simply discouraged – it was considered evil and terrible punishments awaited those who tried to improve themselves educationally. Somaly worked hard in the fields and always came home exhausted. One day, on the way back to the village, she and four other children decided to take a short cut through the cucumber field. It was pouring with rain so they thought that no one would be around to see what they were doing. Since they were hungry, they bent down to pick one cucumber each. Each of the children quickly ate the cucumber since that was not only the easiest but also the nicest way of concealing their 'crime'. As Somaly was stuffing the cucumber into her mouth as fast as she could eat it, she thought of me lying at the house feeling weak. She felt sorry for me and kept a quarter of her cucumber in her pocket for me to eat later. It was a kind thought, but the Khmer Rouge were anxious to stifle all kind thoughts. On the way out of the cucumber field, the five children were stopped by the Khmer Rouge for a spot check. The other four were allowed to run off after being searched, but the Khmer Rouge had quickly found the small piece of cucumber which Somaly had hidden for me. They led Somaly off to a different part of the village which terrified her and she wondered what they would do to her. They gave her a lecture about the evil of her 'crime' and then said that they would beat her up as a punishment. Someone came and told me that Somaly had been arrested, so I ran to where she was being held and pleaded with them to free her. The Khmer Rouge turned on me and told me off, saying that I didn't know how to teach my child to be a good citizen of the new wonderful revolutionary society. I quickly admitted my fault and said that I would instruct my children better in the future. Reluctantly, they agreed to let Somaly go. I grabbed hold of the trembling hand of my daughter and walked away quickly before they could change their minds.

As difficult as life sometimes seemed, it was nothing to what awaited us. Like the Old Testament plagues, which were visited upon the people of Israel, sickness swept over the entire village. First came malaria, which often turned out to be cerebral malaria from which very few recovered.

The malaria got into the brain and the victim quickly went into a coma. Only modern medicines could have saved people, but there were none available. During this time I prayed that God would spare us from the terrible suffering which we saw all around us. When the malaria finally abated, a new sickness came to trouble us. Sores, which rapidly became infected, started to break out on people's legs. These tropical ulcers quickly turned into deep wounds which were as much as 3 – 4 inches wide. There was the smell of rotting flesh everywhere and some people's toes even dropped off. At night we could hear people moaning and children screaming with pain. No one had any explanation for it, although it was clearly a jungle disease. The original inhabitants of the village were not affected, as they appeared to have a natural immunity. Only the 'new' people from the outside, such as ourselves, suffered. Again I prayed that the Lord would deliver us from this plague. Amazingly enough, only my youngest sister was seriously affected. On one ankle the flesh swelled and then began to rot until the wound was three inches across and about half an inch deep. I had a small wound about one inch wide on the back of my right foot, but it was not too serious. Mother prepared some traditional remedies with which she covered the wounds.

The third and final sickness which struck the village was even more terrifying in the way that it hit us. We called it the sleeping sickness, because people simply fell asleep, passed into a coma for one day and then died. The family in the hut next to ours contained eight people. Six of them died, one after the other, within a six-day period until there were only two children left. It appeared that the disease was contagious and we worried constantly that it would spread to our household. Some people had the idea of spreading lime to prevent the spread of the disease, but there was no lime available. We thought of moving elsewhere, but the Khmer Rouge would not allow that. They did nothing to help those who were sick. They only came to look and, then, to help bury the dead. At night we were afraid to sleep, worrying that we would never wake up. After a hard day's work, it was hard to fend off sleep, but I never went to sleep without spending a few moments in silent prayer to God. When we awoke in the early hours of the morning, there was always the strange feeling, "Am I alive or dead?" Once the individual was assured that he himself was alive, then it was time to check the other family members to see if they also were alive. This epidemic only lasted for about a month, but it killed several dozen people. Everyone sighed with relief when it finally abated, and I thanked God for His love and protection for all of my family. It was a sobering thought to realise how close we had all come to death. The only thing that remained to remind me of those terrible weeks was a sore on my foot which had still not completely cleared up.

Harvest time was still continuing and I had to go out into the fields again. Everyone who could walk was mobilised for the harvest as so many of the village had died during those weeks of sickness. There was still water in many of the paddy fields as we waded in to begin the harvest. The sore on my right foot was quite deep and I knew that it would attract the leeches which were quite prevalent in that area. The realisation of this did not encourage me to go into the water, but the choice between leeches and angry Khmer Rouge soldiers was an easy one to make. Before I went into the water, I wrapped my foot very tightly with a strip of material. I reasoned that it would be impossible for a leech to penetrate the material. In fact I tied it so tightly that I could hardly walk. Anyway I preferred that pain to the thought of a leech clinging on to me. We started work on some fields, of which a few were dry whereas others had already been flooded with water. In the flooded fields, I ran from one side to the other, gathering bunches of rice stems which other women had cut, and then carrying them to pile on the dykes around the field. By so doing, I hoped that the leeches would not have enough time to cling on.

However, later on in a new field, I was not allowed to do the same job and was forced to stay with my feet submerged while I began the laborious process of cutting the rice with my small sickle. From time to time, I lifted up my right foot to check that there were no leeches attached to it. To begin with, it seemed like almost every minute. However, little by little I felt safer as I realised that there were no leeches attacking me. Fortunately, there were enough other people in the field to provide an adequate meal for the leeches.

When working in mud and water, one's feet become buried in the mud and this causes an itchy sensation. After a while both my feet became itchy. I put it down to a normal sensation and kept on working. About an hour before lunch, my right foot was so itchy around the wound that I could not resist the temptation to lean down and scratch it. As my hand touched the outside of the tight cloth bandage which I had wrapped around the sore, I felt something soft moving inside the quarter-inch deep sore. The realisation suddenly struck me – it was a leech. A feeling of horror and revulsion overwhelmed me. As I looked down, I could see a large lump under the cloth. In my mind I could imagine the leech with its head buried in my flesh sucking my blood. I couldn't stand it. I screamed at the top of my voice. The screams went on and on as I panicked. All the other workers turned around and stared, wondering if someone was being murdered. I started running, heading straight for the dyke around the paddy field where there was dry ground. As I ran, I screamed and my arms went round and round like a windmill. I was still carrying the sickle and was a danger to anyone who came near me. A Khmer Rouge man came running over to see what the problem was. I screamed, "It's a leech," but I was out of my mind with the horror of what was happening. One man grabbed my arm and snatched the sickle away so that I wouldn't harm someone. Another man grabbed my leg and forced me to sit down. Two women came over and each held an arm to stop me thrashing around. To get the leech out, the man had first to undo the cloth bandage. This took him quite a while because I had tied it so tightly. He finally got it off and, as I looked down at my foot, my horror became real. There was not one leech, but three. Their heads were inside the wound sucking the blood while their tails waved outside as the man was trying to pull them out. They had absorbed so much blood that they were each as big as my thumb. The wound looked twice as big as when I had looked at it that morning. The man pulled on the leeches, but he could not get a proper grip. They were much too slippery and my blood mixed with water and mud made it even more difficult. The pain was excruciating as every attempt to pull the leeches simply made them bite more tightly.

Seeing the commotion and realising what was going on, two of the other women came over. They had a habit of chewing a combination of betel leaves, areca nut, tobacco and lime. One of the women took a wad of this mixture out of her mouth and squeezed it over the wound. This was the best method for getting rid of leeches. The only other way is to burn them off. The leeches partly released their grip and the man was finally able to pull them off. My face was soaked with tears and my throat was sore from all my screaming. I was exhausted and fell back on to the ground.

The Khmer Rouge man got up and said: "OK, now you can go back to work." I looked at him in utter disbelief. The horror of the leeches was still with me and nothing would have dragged me back into the water at that moment. I replied: "You'll have to kill me first. I'm not going back in the water." I was trembling with fear, both of the leeches and of the gun which the Khmer Rouge man waved menacingly in my direction. Seeing me trembling, he must have felt sorry for me, for he turned his back and walked away saying nothing. I sat for a while, feeling worried that the Khmer Rouge might come behind me and shoot me. Usually they said that if a person is still afraid of leeches, then he is too weak to be a good follower of the revolution. Fortunately, lunch-time soon arrived and I was able to merge with the other villagers.

After lunch I was forced to go back into the water. I approached one of the women leaders and begged her to allow me to collect the bunches of rice stems again. She allowed me to do this and it meant that I could move all the time as well as spend some time on the dry land of the dyke. When I had to go into the water, I ran as fast as I could. Thus, the Khmer Rouge were quite satisfied with the pace of my work. I was very thankful for being allowed to do that job, but all the running took my breath away and made me feel very tired. Each day I tried to do the same job, but there were times when I had to harvest as well. As the season continued, the field began to dry up and so it became less of a problem.

From time to time, I was asked by the Khmer Rouge to stay at home in the village to make hats. This was a big privilege, but I had become well-known for the quality of my hats. It had started when I had had some spare time and I recalled some of the things that I had been taught at Teacher Training College. I collected together some of the palm leaves and cut them to shape. Then I sewed them together in the shape of a nice hat. People were always short of hats as they were needed for protection from the sun and the rain. As I continued to make them, my skill increased and I was able to make nicer hats than some of the other women. Then I began to add little decorations to the hats to make them even more attractive. Many people made hats, but the decorations made my hats stand out from other people's. Soon I was besieged with orders for hats. I could not charge people for my efforts because that was against the rules of the Angkar. However, those who wanted hats knew that they needed to offer a small gift in exchange. Otherwise, their hats would never be finished. This might sound mean on my part, but I needed to spend the small amount of spare time available to me for those who would give me a little food in exchange. This extra work increased the supply of food available for my family and we were able to enjoy extra rice, fish, fruit, vegetables and even eggs.

The decorations on the hats varied according to whom the hat was for and were made from rather old brightly-coloured cloth which I collected at every opportunity. Sometimes, I even exchanged food for material which I knew would enhance the look of my hats. I often used to make flowers to sew on to the sides of hats for girls. I even embroidered names on to the sides of hats and this was most popular with the men. I praised God for giving me an education which enabled me to adapt and to think clearly enough to dream up new ideas.

My improved relations with the Khmer Rouge almost lulled me into a false sense of security. I forgot how cruel they could be until an incident took place while we were out in the forest soon after the harvest. We had gone out in a large group to cut grass which would be dried for weaving later into thatch. A number of Khmer Rouge came with us to supervise the operation. Somewhere in the forest the Khmer Rouge arrested a teenage boy who had escaped from some distant village and was making his way to the Thai border. As we all gathered around to see what was happening, the Khmer Rouge began hurling questions at him. He was only 17 and was trembling with fear. When they asked him why he was trying to escape, he replied: "I don't believe that you can build a country just by planting rice. Besides I like studying, so I want to go to Thailand to finish my education." The Khmer Rouge laughed at him. "Don't worry," they said, "we'll send you away to study." The boy was encouraged and looked a little happier, although still unsure of what he had heard. They took him away and locked him up for the night.

The following morning we watched as the Khmer Rouge tied his arms behind his back and two of them led him off into the forest. One man led the way and the other followed carrying on his shoulder a large machete which is usually used for cutting one's way through the forest, and which the Khmer Rouge carried around with them everywhere they went. To begin with, we thought that they were just escorting the boy to the Angkar Loeu, but two hours later the two Khmer Rouge returned alone. One man carried the machete which was still partly red with blood. He had not even bothered to clean it properly. They began to talk to other Khmer Rouge men, but loud enough so that all of us could hear what they were saying. They wanted this to be a lesson to everyone not to try and escape. They described in grisly detail how they had murdered that poor boy by hacking at him with the machete. None of us could contemplate an escape after that.

As the next rainy season approached, my fear of leeches returned and I began to get worried. At the same time we heard a rumour that some people were going to be transferred to a new place. I was extremely happy to hear about it. However, other people became afraid and worried about what the new place would be like. Some people cried and begged the Khmer Rouge to let them stay.

The day of moving eventually arrived. The previous evening, 50 ox-carts had come to the village and we had been told to get everything ready for departure at 4 a.m. the following morning. Some people spent their evening going round to say goodbye to friends in the village. I decided that I could better use my time by talking to the ox-cart drivers and finding out what lay ahead of us. I needed to know what sort of things we should take with us and I also wanted to prepare myself mentally for the future. As I talked to the different men, I got to know one man who asked me why I was asking such questions. I told him about my blind mother and why I needed to be prepared for possible difficulties ahead. I invited him back to our one-room hut for some herbal tea and to share our simple meal. The following morning we didn't have to rush to find an ox-cart because that driver brought his cart over to our hut and even helped us to load it up. He also allowed Mother and Panita to ride on the cart and the rest of us walked alongside. It was a fresh, cool morning as we passed out of the village and I breathed a sigh of relief. I began to smile and said goodbye to Svay Sar for ever.

9 "Think fast or die"

There was no real road to Thmar Pouk, the next stop for us – just a little track that ran through the forest. Occasionally, the track broke through into a clearing and we passed a small village. Some of the little children came running out to see the convoy of ox-carts as we passed by. The adults and the other children were all out working in the fields.

The Khmer 'winter' was over and we were moving into the hottest part of the dry season. However, we were approaching the time for the mango showers. This was a short period of time when brief rains fell and made the mango flowers blossom. Without these rains, the season for mangoes (a soft juicy fruit when it ripens) would have been very poor. Seeing the approach of the showers, I was able to estimate that it was around March 1978. Since we worked seven days a week and had no watches or calendars, we easily lost track of time. We only knew the year as it was divided up into the different seasons.

It had been raining the previous night and the path was not too hot to walk on. When we were finally allowed to stop and cook our lunch, there was no water source nearby and so we had to scoop the water from the muddy puddles of rain-water in order to drink and to have water with which to cook our rice. It was very gritty from the mud and made our rice rather crunchy. In normal circumstances, I would have been horrified to eat such a concoction. However, at that time we were only too thankful that the Khmer Rouge had stopped to let us cook and eat.

After lunch, we began our journey again. Eventually, my feet started to blister, since I was not wearing any shoes even though I had a pair of Khmer Rouge sandals. These were made out of rubber taken from car tyres. The straps holding the sandals on to one's feet were made from the inner tubes of the tyres. They were called Khmer Rouge sandals because the Khmer Rouge had used them widely during their war with Lon Nol's forces. My sandals were too heavy to walk in for very far and so I carried them over my shoulder. With the blisters and my general state of exhaustion, I sat down many times to rest. Little by little I lost sight of Mother and Panita on the cart. I struggled on and arrived at Thmar Pouk at almost 6 p.m. I was directed to a temple which was devoid of any monks. The Khmer Rouge believed in no religion except the power of the Angkar. All the monks had been disrobed and had been sent to work in the fields like everyone else.

I met up with the rest of my family and we were all sent to a large hall which had previously been part of the temple complex. One person from each family was asked to go to a meeting right away. There, a Khmer Rouge leader came and gave a political speech which was more or less the same thing that had been told to us before. He exhorted us to support the Angkar and extolled the glories of the revolution. Then he asked if we whole-heartedly agreed to follow the Angkar. As usual, we had to close our right fist, lift it high in the air and shout loudly together, "Phdach-nha, phdach-nha!", which means "We're determined to do so". The lecture ended with the Khmer Rouge leader asking us to donate any gold that we still possessed so that we could become good members of the revolution. This was supposed to loosen our ties with the past and make us ready to accept the new order. It was also to let us know that if anyone was found with gold later on, they would be in serious trouble.

A few people responded and gave some of their gold to the Khmer Rouge. I imagine that this was out of fear in case they were discovered with the gold later on. I still had some pieces of gold and jewellery which I had carefully concealed in my clothing. Although I was fearful that they might be discovered if the Khmer Rouge conducted a body search on us all, I was prepared to risk that danger because I knew that I would need my valuables to continue buying food from the Khmer Rouge for my family in the future. The token amount of gold offered up to the Khmer Rouge was obviously not satisfactory, so they announced that they would send someone back to the main hall to check our bags and other belongings. Since we had already indicated by our silence that we didn't have any more gold, they would consider anything which they found as belonging to the Angkar. The people at the meeting were asked to stay on while some of the Khmer Rouge went off to search our bags in the large hall.

I had no valuables in my bags – nor was there anything else in the bags of the rest of my family, so I was not unduly concerned. However, in one of my bags was an Oxford English Dictionary which I had saved since I left Phnom Penh. It sounds absurd to have risked my life for it, but somehow it was really precious to me. I used to read it in secret during my free time as if it was a novel and it was my link with the world I had known before the fall of Phnom Penh. In other villages, the Khmer Rouge had searched my house and belongings many times. Each time I had asked God to keep the dictionary safe and it had never yet been discovered.

Now, as the Khmer Rouge went off to search our bags, leaving us seated there, I prayed: "Please, Lord, make their eyes blind. Don't let them see my dictionary." I was not so much concerned about the loss of the dictionary as what its discovery would mean to me and my family. With the Khmer Rouge's hatred of the educated classes, it could spell death for me. A little later, the search was finished and the Khmer Rouge came back with a box full of gold and jewellery. Some had been found buried in rice, some sewn into cloth patches on clothes and even some hidden on people's bodies. No mention was made of the original owners, since they could not identify which bag belonged to whom, and we were all allowed to go. I returned to the large hall and found my mother sitting in the middle of all our bags. I asked Mother if she knew where my bag with the dictionary was, but of course she couldn't tell me since she was blind. I looked everywhere, but the bag was gone. Saddened, I looked around fearfully to see if the Khmer Rouge were coming to find out who was the owner of the book. No one was heading my way, so I set about organising the cooking of our supper since it was already getting late in the evening. Later on, I took Panita out into the bushes to relieve herself. As we came back to the hall, I lifted one foot to climb on to the hall floor, which was slightly raised off the ground. As I did so, my foot struck something just under the floor. Bending down, I picked it up and, to my joy, discovered that it was the bag with my dictionary inside. It was physically impossible for it to have either rolled or been thrown there. My family had been sitting well inside the hall and, anyway, none of them knew anything about my bag being missing. Yet there it was, and I praised God for His seemingly miraculous intervention.

The following morning, several dozen ox-carts came at 6 a.m. to where we were sleeping. Each village in that area had sent about ten ox-carts to help the people carry their belongings to their new village. The leader from each set of ox-carts came round all the families to choose the ones who would go with them. As soon as they realised that there were no strong men in our family, they passed us by. They were also put off by the fact that Mother was blind and my sister, Sokhon, who now had a baby, was quite sick. We were one of the last families to be chosen, but finally at noon we joined a group on their way to a village called Andoeung Klong. It was only about two kilometres outside the district town of Thmar Pouk, so it did not take us long to arrive there.

Upon arrival we were given lunch by the village canteen. The canteen leader took one look at our family and shook her head in disgust. I heard later that she said it was a waste to feed such a family since we all looked too thin to be able to do any work. We were given a house to live in together with Sokhon's family, and were all ordered to report for work the next day. Somehow, I sensed that I could be happier here than I had been in Svay Sar. The people seemed to be more civilised and to have had the benefit of some education. Like the Svay Sar people, they were kind and seemed even more friendly. Although they were totally under the control of the Khmer Rouge, yet they seemed to have learned how to exist under their rule without giving their hearts to the revolutionary movement. The work was just as hard, but we received enough food and we were better treated. There seemed to be less fear in the atmosphere in spite of our close proximity to the main district headquarters of the Khmer Rouge in Thmar Pouk. I gradually learned to accept this way of life, which didn't appear too bad at that point, and it certainly appeared that the new society was there to stay. I had stopped thinking consciously about the future. My daily weariness allowed me to think only of how to get enough food to survive the next day.

As in every other village, I went out to work in the fields during the day. By evening I was quite tired and yet I forced myself to go into the canteen, which was right next door to our house, and offer to help them voluntarily. A new leader had been appointed for the canteen and it was much easier for me to get on with her. I helped them to chop up some of the food ready for cooking or distribution very early the next morning. Little by little I was asked to help with the calculations of how much food we needed to go and ask for from the District Cooperative. The food was used to feed our group, and we used different amounts each day as the numbers fluctuated fairly frequently, because of people who came back to see their family from time to time. Although people were often assigned to work stations far from the village, they could occasionally get permission from the Khmer Rouge to come back for a short visit. It was quite simple to calculate the changes and was very easy for me. I took over the task of inventory and stock control, which had taxed the minds of those to whom it had been assigned. Through my voluntary work there, I was often able to glean some extra food for my family. This was possible either by scraping up some of the rice that had stuck to the bottom of the pots or by scraping the inside of a sugar sack to get out the last grains of sugar. In addition, I was able to build up a good relationship with the canteen leader and, because of my ability to assist her in most tasks and to control the food efficiently, I was later appointed to be the assistant to the canteen leader, which meant that I didn't have to go to work in the fields under the burning sun.

I was overjoyed at this promotion. It was a plum job and many people would have liked to have traded places with me. It was an important position in the village and I took great care to do everything correctly since I did not want to lose the job. Nearly every day I was sent to the District Cooperative of Thmar Pouk, which was only a little more than two kilometres away, to collect some supplies for our canteen. During my visits there, I got to know the chief of the Cooperative, who was second in importance only to the district chief of the Khmer Rouge. One day he asked me if I knew anyone who could sew as he needed someone to repair the clothes of the people who went out to the fields to work. They had no time to repair their own clothes at night. I told him that I could do a little sewing and he asked me if I would like to go to work in the Cooperative as the sewing woman. I wasn't really sure if I wanted to do that job as I was fairly comfortable in my current job in the canteen and I saw no reason to switch. I declined his offer as gracefully as I could without offending him and continued working in the canteen at Andoeung Klong.

A few months later, the people from my original group became envious of what seemed like an easy way of life for me and went to see the village chief, asking him to send me back to work in the fields with them and he agreed. The work in the fields was much harder, and there was less food available, so my health began to deteriorate again. One day, when I was sick, I got permission to go to the hospital in Thmar Pouk for treatment. On the way back I stopped at the District Cooperative and found that the sewing job, at which I had turned up my nose earlier, had still not been filled. I went to see the Cooperative chief, and offered my services. He accepted me for the job immediately and made arrangements with the leader in Andoeung Klong for me to go to work there every day. Once again life became a little more pleasant for me, but it was not to last.

Two months went by and it was announced that the Angkar needed several families to be sent into the rural areas beyond Thmar Pouk where there was a lot of uncultivated land and where they were short of labour. Each group consisted of about 20 families consisting of both 'new' people and villagers, and the Khmer Rouge decided to choose the groups to go by drawing pieces of paper out of a hat. The first few groups whose pieces of paper were drawn from the hat were ordered to pack up and leave. Unfortunately, our group was among them. I knew for sure that life would be more difficult going back into the countryside, but I had no choice in the matter. On the day of departure, the men from all the families ran out to locate ox-carts to carry their belongings. We had already packed but we had to wait a long time until we were able to find an ox-cart that would take us. As a result, we were one of the last families to arrive in the new village of Trar Yoeung. The others had all been able to locate nice houses in the centre of the village and there was nothing left for us. We were directed to a house some way outside the village and it seemed as if it was situated in the middle of the forest. However, the hospitality afforded us by the owner greatly relieved the feeling of isolation which we at first felt.

The work was very similar to that which we had experienced in other villages. Depending on the season, we were given the task of planting rice, digging canals, clearing the forest or cutting grass for thatch. During the lunch-break, I ate quickly so that I had enough time to go to the nearby river and fish. We had a small net which was shaped like a big bag and which could be pulled along by two people holding a stick at either side. I had purchased it in Svay Sar with one ounce of gold which I had saved from Phnom Penh. It was worth much more than that to us now as we were able to add considerably to our diet. That net made the difference between my family being adequately fed and going hungry.

Whenever life was going reasonably well, something would happen to disrupt things. The current Khmer Rouge leader of our group, who was a woman, came and said to me: "Everyone in our new society must be equal. It is not fair that you should have a net while other people do not have one. You must place your net in the canteen, so that it becomes the property of the whole group. That way, everyone can benefit and not only you." This eminently fair-sounding statement struck a chord with me as I had no wish to stand out from everyone else nor to be thought badly of by them. I gave up my net and it was placed in the canteen, where anyone could go and ask for it. However, I never again had an opportunity to use my net and, before long, it disintegrated through over-use and lack of care.

It was not long before I discovered that there were several others in our group who had bigger and better nets than our family and who had been allowed to keep them for personal use. It seemed strange to me that this should be so, and I discreetly asked around as to the reason. Its simplicity stunned and angered me. The net owners had been allowed to keep their nets because they paid a small bribe in the form of fish to the group leader.

As I thought about it all, I realised that the communist system under the Khmer Rouge might sound fine in theory, because everyone should have been treated equally and it was supposed to have been clean and incorruptible. However, in practice it was the same as other systems that we had experienced in Cambodia. No system that is imposed upon a people from the outside can work unless the people themselves are in agreement with it. In other words, every system – be it benign dictatorship, communism or democracy – is dependent upon the people themselves. A system, even a democracy where individuals are able to make their own choices, cannot change people – the people themselves have to change, and that can only come about through a change of heart of the sort that I had experienced when I became a Christian, when one thinks first of others before oneself.

My sewing reputation from Thmar Pouk had come with me to this new village. Since the village Cooperative had just received some mosquito netting material, they needed someone to sew it up into nets. To my great delight I was asked to do the sewing. There was enough netting to make one or two nets for each family, depending on the number of people in the family. This took quite a while and life became a little easier for me as I worked away in the Cooperative building. During food distribution times, I stopped sewing and went to help with the division of the food. It meant that I was again able to scrape up small amounts of extra food to take back to my family so that once more we had enough to eat.

It was at about this time that we began to hear rumours of fighting along the Cambodian border with Vietnam. We were unable to glean very much information from the Khmer Rouge, but little bits of news kept filtering along the 'underground' information network. The Vietnamese border was a long way from where we were and we were unaware of the seriousness of the fighting. One of the results, however, was that we received a new Khmer Rouge chief.

One day I was told to go and visit the District Cooperative in Thmar Pouk to collect some material. It was about three kilometres to Thmar Pouk and I was allowed to take Somaly with me to help carry back the sewing material. We had a nice time walking there and for once we felt a little bit free. Arriving at the Cooperative, I began to collect together the material that was needed in Trar Yoeung. At one point I looked up and noticed a young man staring at me. As he looked into my eyes, his face lit up with recognition and he came straight over. He addressed me with a happy voice: "Neak Krou,[1] you're still alive." I was startled and my shock must have been apparent. I had hoped that I had been successful in concealing my former identity, but here was one of my old students who had recognised me and who had inadvertently given me away. It was exactly the same situation that had led to the disappearance of my brother, An. Was I now to share the same fate?

A Khmer Rouge man sitting nearby immediately turned to me and said: "Oh, so you were a teacher!" The enormity of the situation had yet to sink into my brain, which was still n.mb with shock. I responded by saying rather

---

[1] 'Neak Krou' is the Khmer word for teacher. In Cambodia, students didn't call their teachers or lecturers by name, but simply addressed them as 'Teacher'.

innocently, "What?" My ex-student realised immediately what he had done and his face registered a mixture of fear and regret. I began to understand that I was in serious trouble and a chill ran up my spine. I thought to myself: "Think fast, or you're going to die. Lord, only you can help me out of this situation." I said another "What?" to give myself more time to think. The face of the Khmer Rouge man began to darken and my knees began to tremble. Since I had worked in the District Cooperative before, I felt almost at home in the place and was not awed by my surroundings. I suddenly felt emboldened and smiled at the Khmer Rouge man: "Wait a minute. Do you think I'm a school teacher? I'm not – I'm a fortune-teller!"

The Lord had cleared my brain enough for me to remember that the Khmer word for teacher is also used to describe a fortune-teller. I continued: "If you don't believe me, ask this young man." I pointed to my ex-student and prayed that he would take his cue and respond accordingly. To my relief, he backed me up and said: "That's right, she's a fortune-teller." The Khmer Rouge man looked doubtful and probably thought that I was trying to trick him. He said: "If you're really a fortune-teller, read my palm." He held out his hand and I nearly fainted. Now I was really on the spot as I had never done any fortune-telling in my life.

Pretending to wipe the sweat off my forehead, I bent my head and prayed: "Lord, help me to say the right thing which will please him." I had to cast my memory back to things which I had tried to forget. I had tried to wipe out so much of the past in my mind to avoid betraying myself inadvertently to the Khmer Rouge by my actions or by the things that I said. Now it was time to remember the psychology that I had studied at Teacher Training College. I was also helped by the fact that I had associated with the many visitors and soldiers in my father's house, who came from working-class backgrounds. I had got to know many of them and knew the way that they thought and behaved in life. As I searched the depths of my mind, memories came flashing back. Before I became a Christian, I had read a book on astrology and had even visited a fortune-teller on a few occasions. I could picture the old fortune-teller in my mind and, suddenly, I knew what to say. "Thank you, Lord," I breathed and took the outstretched hand of the Khmer Rouge man. As I began to talk to him, I watched his face intently. I was able to judge by his eye and head movements as to whether I was saying the right things or not. If he reacted well to a sentence, then I continued on the same theme. If he didn't seem pleased with the direction of my speaking, I changed the topic. I could tell from the roughness of his hand and the accent of his voice from which background and way of life he came. The words that he used and his behaviour told me more about him and I used this information to extract more details of his personal life from him. I was able to build on that to tell him more about himself. After about five minutes he began to smile and became more friendly. Once again, the Lord had come to my rescue in my time of need.

After that, I began to acquire a reputation for fortune-telling and many people came to ask me to read their palms. I tried to tell people that I really wasn't very good, but still they came. Eventually, I came to look on it as a joke and was able to laugh about it. Sometimes, people were so impressed by my 'accuracy' that they would bring small gifts of food. It would have been churlish to have refused and it helped to fill the hungry bellies of my family.

Having collected all the material from the Cooperative, Somaly and I put it together in a large pile and realised that we would have a struggle to carry it all back to Trar Yoeung. At that point the Cooperative chief came along and saw our difficulty. He came over to talk with us and then offered to lend us a bicycle to carry everything back to the village. It was very kind of him, as normally only the Khmer Rouge were allowed to use bicycles. We loaded things up on the back and set off for the village. Somaly walked in front and occasionally I rode the bicycle to avoid having to push it the whole way. We had only gone about 500 metres out of Thmar Pouk when the pathway narrowed to pass along the top of a dyke between two paddy-fields. Somaly was some way ahead and I decided to ride the bicycle to catch up with her. As I neared the narrowest part of the path, I began to wobble and the top-heavy bicycle started to tilt to one side. I felt myself falling and crashed heavily on my left shoulder. I felt something snap inside and knew that my collar-bone was broken. I couldn't move my arm and the bicycle had fallen across my body. I was in such pain that I couldn't even call Somaly.

After a while, a man came along the track and saw me lying there. I called out to him to help me, but he refused. I couldn't believe it and asked him why. He said it was against the rules of the Angkar for a man and a woman to be alone together in a quiet place. He walked away from me leaving me speechless and writhing in pain.

I tried to call out to Somaly to come back and help me. However, she was a long way ahead and my feeble shouts didn't reach her. It was some time before she realised that I was not behind her. Then she turned and ran back to me. Somaly helped me to get up and to put my arm in a sling by using a kramar, which is a piece of material unique to Cambodia and can be used for almost any purpose. Together we then managed to get the bicycle up again and, while I steadied it with my right hand and nursed my injured arm, Somaly pushed it the rest of the way back to Thmar Pouk. The bicycle was quite big, with a heavy load, while Somaly was still small. It seemed incredible to me that she managed to find the strength to push it all the way back to the village. We left the bicycle and its load at the first house in the village that we came to.

There was no medicine to help dull the pain, and I had to put up with it. Since nobody there could do anything to help me with my broken collar-bone, I decided to walk back to Trar Yoeung with Somaly before it became dark. Upon my arrival in the village, I reported the accident to the village chief and I was allowed to stay at home for one week while my collar-bone began to heal. Then I was sent back to work in the village Cooperative. I still could not do any sewing, but I helped a little with the food distribution.

Very late one afternoon, I was sitting by the window of the Cooperative doing some sewing when I noticed a commotion going on nearby. The village chief was using a large stick to beat a young man. The blows rained down on the body of the man as the chief cursed him for his 'crime' of 'stealing' a few grains of rice from the edge of the field. The sight sickened me but there was nothing that I could do. It had become almost an everyday occurrence and I tried to ignore the screams of pain. What I did notice was that several people kept looking at me and then looking at the young man. It finally penetrated that this was Peauv, my youngest brother. I was paralysed with fear and felt myself powerless to intervene. A moment later, I think someone must have told the village chief that the boy was my brother, as I saw him looking over in my direction, and he stopped the beating. I had always got on well with the village chief because, apart from working hard, I used to help his wife at home during my spare time. He walked back into the Cooperative and simply said, in a very low voice: "I didn't realise that he was your brother."

I said nothing, wondering if I should ask him to let me go outside to help my brother who was lying half-dead on the ground in his dusty torn clothes. However, I knew it was against the Angkar philosophy to want to help some-one, even my brother, who had been caught doing some-thing wrong. My heart ached from not being able even to cry for him. Several minutes later, he dragged himself back home and realised that he had one rib broken. Peauv should have rested at home, but he went back to work the next day. He didn't dare let the Khmer Rouge think that he was lazy. He was only thankful that the Khmer Rouge had spared his life the previous evening.

Later in December 1978, the harvest season had begun and the Khmer Rouge were pushing us every day to speed up the harvest. The rumours of approaching war grew stronger and we felt the urgency to finish gathering in the crop. I no longer worked in the Cooperative, but went out to work in the fields with everyone else. Even the chief of the Cooperative worked in the fields by day and in the Cooperative in the evening. At night we often worked until 11 p.m. or midnight, threshing the rice which had been harvested during the day. Even the young children and mothers with small babies were organised into groups to work.

The village chief appointed me to be the leader of a group of about 500 people. This was composed mainly of women with babies and elderly people. I was responsible for ensuring that they had enough to eat and that they got up in time to work. If they were sick, I had to make sure that they weren't pretending and that they were taken to the clinic. It was a difficult job to manage all these different people. At night we were not allowed to return to our homes in the village. We slept in the fields curled up under the stars. It was hard for me because I was separated from my family. Somaly was away working in a children's group, while Panita was back in the village helping to take care of Mother.

By appointing me as a group leader, the village chief had set a precedent. All the other leaders were 'old' people. They had lived with the Khmer Rouge since well before the fall of Phnom Penh. However, I was one of the 'new' people who had been forced to become part of the revolution. It created bad feelings among the other leaders and they were afraid of an erosion of their privileges. They constantly complained that I didn't know how to do my job properly and said that I should be replaced.

One evening, while assisting with the threshing, I went to see the village chief intending to discuss something about the next day's work. As I approached the pile of hay near where he was sitting, I noticed that he was deep in conversation with one of the other group leaders. I decided to wait until they had finished so that I would not interrupt them. I sat down on the other side of the pile of hay. Since a number of people were moving around, my presence was not particularly noticed by the two men. Their conversation drifted over to me in snatches and I heard my name mentioned. My ears pricked up and I edged closer to hear what they were saying. The other group leader was saying that he had heard that I was a capitalist and that I had been a teacher before. He said that the Angkar should not keep such people. His words and the tone of voice that he used made it sound as if he was suggesting that I should be eliminated. The village chief made no comment and I crept away feeling shocked. I must have looked pale and distraught, but it was dark and no one noticed that I was shaking with fear. After the work was finished, I went home and lay down. Sleep eluded me and I prayed all through the night. I wondered if I would be taken away in the morning. All sorts of nasty images were conjured up in my mind. Who would take care of my children and my blind mother if I was killed?

The next morning, I went to see the Khmer Rouge deputy chief whose wife had been especially friendly to me. I told them exactly what I had heard the previous night. I was so distressed that I sobbed it all out through the middle of my tears. I told them that I had worked hard, which proved that I followed the Angkar and was respectful of their rules. I asked if I had done something wrong and pointed out that the Angkar had said that the 'new' people would be accepted if they changed their ways. The Khmer

Rouge couple tried to comfort me and said that everyone knew that I was a hard worker. The husband was sure that the village chief would not listen to the other group leader and counselled me to go back to work as if nothing had happened. He said that he was sure he could work things out. I wiped away my tears and walked off without really seeing where I was going.

Nothing serious happened, but the other leaders put pressure on me to resign. I knew that I could not resign, or I would be seen as refusing work given to me by the Khmer Rouge. It seemed like an impossible situation, but I could see one way out. I went to the village chief and asked him if I could be transferred to a model group comprised only of efficient unmarried women. This was an élite group that worked very hard and, in effect, I was saying to the village chief that I wanted to work harder. It was a convenient excuse for me to leave my other responsibilities and I was allowed to transfer, which satisfied the other leaders since I was now an ordinary member of a group.

Now, as we harvested in the fields, we could hear artillery fire in the distance. The rumours of war had come true and we all realised that heavy fighting was taking place not very far away. The Khmer Rouge began to become nervous. They told everyone that the Vietnamese had invaded and were trying to swallow Cambodia. We were told that we were expected to sacrifice ourselves to save Cambodia and to defend our country against Vietnam. Secretly, we hoped that the Vietnamese would be successful and save us from the mindless terror that had gripped our country for the past four years. This might sound very unpatriotic to anyone who has not lived through those terrible years, but at the time I felt that nothing could be worse than the Khmer Rouge and that any change had to be a change for the better. The years that we had spent in the different villages had been hard for us. On several occasions, I thought that my time to die had come. Somehow, most of us had survived, but I didn't know how much longer we could continue under such conditions.

The Khmer Rouge started to load up their families and belongings into ox-carts and to move out. The last orders which we were given were that the whole village had to move back to Thmar Pouk. The Khmer Rouge told us that there was still much rice to be harvested there. It seemed strange, but we were programmed to obey orders. There were no ox-carts left, for they had all been taken by the Khmer Rouge and families with strong men. We bundled up our possessions and began the three-kilometre walk back to Thmar Pouk.

10 Out of the Frying-Pan . . .

When the Khmer Rouge took over Phnom Penh in April 1975, many greeted the incoming guerrillas as saviours and welcomed the end of the war. However, the longed-for peace never came to our beloved country. The suffering that we had experienced during the five-year civil war, and from which we longed to escape, continued worse than before. Now war had come once more to ravage our beautiful homeland. While we slaved in the fields of Battambang, thinking that we were helping to rebuild our country, the lust of killing never left the minds of the Khmer Rouge. Not content merely to kill their own people, the Khmer Rouge turned against the people of Thailand and even against their former friends, the Vietnamese.

As early as January 1977, the Khmer Rouge began to make cross-border raids into Thailand. They slaughtered many innocent villagers and stole cattle. Later, in a bid to justify their actions to a horrified outside world, the Khmer Rouge claimed that the villages were inside Cambodia and that they were merely rearranging their own internal affairs. It was a frightening statement. Meanwhile, over on the Vietnamese border, the Khmer Rouge decided that they were in danger of being dominated by their former allies. During their struggle against the Lon Nol forces from 1970 to 1975, the Vietnamese had sent large quantities of war material to aid their communist brothers. In addition, they provided training in North Vietnam to many thousands of men who flocked to join the Khmer Rouge when Prince Sihanouk proclaimed himself their friend.

From 1977 onwards, the Khmer Rouge launched raid after raid over the border into different parts of South Vietnam. For a while the Vietnamese put up with it, hoping that they could persuade the Khmer Rouge to toe the fraternal line. However, by 1978 the Vietnamese had had enough. They began to organise an Army of Salvation under the leadership of a man called Heng Samrin, who had been a Khmer Rouge leader before. He had been critical of the central leadership in Phnom Penh and had just escaped with his life, by crossing into Vietnam, when the Khmer Rouge sent loyal troops to conduct a purge. Now the Vietnamese were ready to use him. Little by little, they built up a tiny Khmer invasion army to provide legitimacy to the invasion which was finally led by Vietnamese troops in late 1978. The Vietnamese quickly overran Khmer Rouge positions in the east. By January 7th, 1979, the Vietnamese were in Phnom Penh and were beginning to roll westwards towards the border with Thailand. The Khmer Rouge melted before them and started to drift back to the forests and mountains to begin a protracted guerrilla war. As the Vietnamese approached Thmar Pouk, we were able to hear the sound of artillery growing louder.

Our journey to Thmar Pouk was cut short by the Khmer Rouge while we were still two kilometres from the town. We were ordered to stop and set up camp in the forest. Then the Khmer Rouge soldiers seemed to disappear one after the other – presumably to fight. Only the leaders of each group were left behind to organise things and they sent us into the nearby fields to harvest rice. As we worked, the sound of artillery crept closer and closer. There was no sign of any Khmer Rouge and, after ten days, the sense of being controlled through fear seemed to slip away from us all. Many of the villagers said that we should go on to Thmar Pouk since we had no proper shelter in the fields.

There were no guards and no one in real authority to prevent us, so the people began to leave in small groups. I gathered our family together and we made the short journey to Thmar Pouk in early February.

Some of the people who arrived in the town before us came back out to warn us that there were strange soldiers everywhere. Upon arrival, we found armed men at the entrance of the town and we recognised them immediately as Vietnamese. We understood right away why there were no Khmer Rouge in the area. Were the Vietnamese our enemies, as the Khmer Rouge had tried to drum into us? Or had they come to rescue us from our misery? We were confused and didn't know whether to run back into the forest and hide or to go forward. As we say in Cambodia, we were caught between the tiger on the dry land and the crocodile in the water. Looking about us warily, we moved slowly into Thmar Pouk. It wasn't long before we were able to find an empty house, which we shared with another family.

From then on, there was no one to give us orders. We no longer had any set working hours or tasks to do. However, somehow we had to survive and we went out in search of food. In the fields close to Thmar Pouk, we were able to glean grains of rice from stems which had fallen to the ground during harvest. From our frequent collections, we were able to have more than enough rice to eat, but we continued to be very fearful of what would happen next. The Vietnamese seemed to be friendly towards the civilian population. They threw open the doors of the Khmer Rouge storehouses and people were allowed to go and ask for anything that they needed. Rice and sugar were distributed and we were at last able to find proper pots and pans to cook with. Many things had been stored by the Khmer Rouge and very little had been given out to the ordinary people.

The people were overjoyed at having been released from

the oppression of four years under the yoke of the Khmer Rouge. There was a feeling of 'salvation' and euphoria. However, I knew that these, too, were soldiers and that above all they had come from another communist country. They seemed helpful today, but what would they be like tomorrow? I remembered back to that fateful day of April 17th, 1975, when we had witnessed the scenes of joy as the Khmer Rouge entered Phnom Penh and at last the war seemed to be over. Were we to be disappointed again in a similar way? For the time being, we made the most of their help and ignored the fact that it was probably a psychological manoeuvre to draw the people away from any possible support for the Khmer Rouge.

Several days went by and we became frustrated with the total lack of information. There were lots of rumours flying round, but we didn't know anything for sure. Were the Vietnamese in full control of the countryside? Had the Khmer Rouge army completely disintegrated or were they regrouping for a counter-attack? In an effort to gain more information, I went to see the Vietnamese officer in charge of the troops who were guarding Thmar Pouk. I discovered that he spoke a little French and I was able to speak a little Vietnamese, which I had picked up from an old Vietnamese cook who had been employed by my mother when I was quite young. Now it came in useful and, with the officer's French and my own knowledge of the French language, we were able to communicate quite successfully. I learned about the fierce fighting that was taking place not very far away and received some words of assurance that, whatever might happen, the Vietnamese would stay to protect us. However, the whole town seemed very quiet, as though it was awaiting something new to happen.

Around mid-February, the Vietnamese suddenly started to make preparations to move out. We began to worry for we were afraid that the Khmer Rouge would take over again. A number of families decided to move out with the

Vietnamese troops and make their way back to Phnom Penh. These were primarily people who had originally lived in Phnom Penh. I wanted to go as well and talked it over with the rest of the family. We all decided that it would be best to leave and to head back to a more familiar environment. We packed up and put all our belongings into a cart the night before.

Before going to sleep that night, a friend of mine, who was a native of that area, came to see me. She said that I should not leave the next day because she felt that the Vietnamese soldiers would be an irresistible target for the Khmer Rouge. "I don't want to stop you from going back to Phnom Penh, but please wait a while and see what happens," she pleaded. I was reluctant to stay and she could see the hesitation in my face. "Look," she said, "I'm not a Christian like you. I'm a Buddhist. Let's light an incense stick and you pray to the God in whom you believe. If the incense stick burns brightly, take it as a sign that you should go to Phnom Penh tomorrow, and if it burns very dimly or fizzles out, then that means that you shouldn't go." I told her that I didn't really believe in seeking guidance in such a manner, but I finally agreed to do it, so that she would leave me alone. We lit a stick and I prayed. By the time that I had finished, the incense stick was extinguished. I was so keen to leave the next day that I presented excuses. "The stick must have been damp," I said. However, my friend was not about to give up. We followed the same procedure five times with a different stick and each time the same thing happened. The stick either burned very dimly or died down. I still insisted on leaving the next morning and my friend left, still pleading with me not to go.

As I lay down to sleep, I continued my prayers, asking God to give me direction. When we awoke early the next morning, I was dismayed to find Peauv doubled over in agony. His stomach was giving him great pain and tears were pouring down his face. I thought about the journey. It would have been hard enough for us to push the cart with just our belongings in it, let alone not having Peauv to help us push it, but it would have been impossible to have pushed it with Peauv sick inside as well. We decided to stay on and I finally felt at peace, realising that this was God's way of ensuring that we did not leave with the rest of the group.

Around midday, someone from the group which had left came staggering back into the town and told us that almost half of the group had been killed by land-mines. The Vietnamese troops had been leading the way. When they had come to a bridge, they had branched off to one side and gone through paddy-fields and part of the forest to by-pass the bridge. Some of the Khmers had followed them, but the vast majority had gone straight over the bridge because they were hampered by the carts with all their belongings. As they went over the bridge, terrible explosions ripped into their bodies. The Khmer Rouge had planted anti-personnel mines, which had been detonated by the tramping of so many feet across the bridge. Many were killed or wounded and there were few able to struggle onwards with the Vietnamese. None of the Vietnamese soldiers had been willing to stay and help the wounded. They were too afraid of a Khmer Rouge ambush. The dead lay where they had fallen and the badly wounded were left to die under the burning sun, since none of those who had escaped the explosion dared to go forward to rescue them for fear of triggering further explosions. As I listened to this story, I knew for sure that God had really had His hand on me and was protecting me.

Shortly after the Vietnamese left, the Khmer Rouge moved back into the town. It was obvious that they had massed their forces around Thmar Pouk and this had forced the Vietnamese to pull back. The town soon became a Khmer Rouge staging post as we saw hundreds of ox-carts moving through laden with goods and accompanied by the families of the Khmer Rouge soldiers. Several trucks also went lumbering off down the road towards the jungles close to the border with Thailand. These were probably full of weapons and ammunition. All of the Khmer Rouge whom we saw looked very distressed. Although they had come back into Thmar Pouk, the sight of their families streaming westwards confirmed that in general they were on the run from the Vietnamese.

The Khmer Rouge presence gave us cause for worry and before long the original Thmar Pouk leaders returned and began to check the population again. A friend in the village came to me with a frightened look on her face and told me to hide because the Khmer Rouge were actively searching for me. Someone had told them that I had got on well with the Vietnamese and the Khmer Rouge were anxious to make an example of, and punish, anyone who had cooperated with the 'enemy'. My friend had told the Khmer Rouge that I had left with the group that had accompanied the Vietnamese troops in the direction of Phnom Penh, and that I had probably been killed then. From then on, I hid in our house for 24 hours a day. It was claustrophobic for me and I knew that I would not be able to endure it for a long period of time. However, capture by the Khmer Rouge at that point would have brought me to the horrible death from which God had so far protected me.

One day, a girl came looking for me. She was from the nearby village of Srae Memai, which was about one kilometre from Thmar Pouk. Holding a bunch of palm leaves, it appeared that she had come to ask me to make her a hat. However, she seemed nervous and her eyes darted everywhere before she entered my house. Then, in a very low voice, she whispered: "Your husband is in Thailand and has sent someone to look for you." My jaw dropped as I took in the implications of what she had said. I had dreamed about him for the last five years, ever since he had gone off to Paris to study in August 1974. I had imagined so many different ways of meeting him and I had pictured a thousand times how I would greet him. Now my dream was about to come true.

My astonishment must have been apparent to the girl, for she nodded her head vigorously and said: "Yes, he's really in Thailand and he has sent someone for you and the children." After the initial reaction of delight, I became a little suspicious. "How does my husband know that I am here?" I asked the girl. She stared back at me with a blank expression. "I'm afraid that I have no idea," she replied, "but if you come with me to Srae Memai, I'm sure that the man from Thailand can tell you." I looked at her for a while, then shook my head and said: "No, I need some kind of proof if I am to risk my life in an escape attempt." She looked crestfallen, but I still suspected that it might be a trick. Several other people had been asked if they wanted to escape. They had been led off into the forest with their 'guide' and had then been robbed of all their possessions. We had even heard of some people who had been killed by their guides. I began to be less eager to go with this young girl. The last that I had heard of my husband was in early 1975, when I knew that he was still in France. However, it could well be true that he had come to Thailand in an attempt to try to locate our daughters and me. I wanted so much to believe that he was there waiting for me, but I was afraid of the deception and terror that could await us in the forest. The girl indicated that I would have to leave that same evening and I seized on that as an excuse. "I cannot possibly be ready in time. My blind mother is here and I cannot leave her right away." The girl went away with a look of disappointment on her face and I wondered if I had done the right thing. That night I talked it over with Mother and she agreed with me that there was a great danger that it could be a trick.

The Khmer Rouge continued to maintain a heavy

presence in Thmar Pouk and I heard from my friends that they were still searching for me. It was becoming difficult to stay hidden all the time and my mind turned constantly to the thought of escape. I told Mother that, if the opportunity presented itself again, I would take the chance and go to Thailand. Mother would not consider the possibility of escaping as her blindness precluded that option. However, she knew that I could not stay in the same situation for long, with the Khmer Rouge constantly on the look out for me.

Several days later, a buffalo belonging to our next-door neighbour became sick and died. We had been without meat for so long that we were ready to eat anything. We ignored the cause of death and I offered to help in the task of cutting up the carcass in the hope that I would be given a small amount of meat at the end. I took a knife and joined in the gory task of slicing great joints of meat off the bone. Much of it would be tough to eat, but at least it was meat. At one stage, the point of the knife I was using nicked the back of my right hand. It was more of a scratch than a cut, but it began to itch soon after. With all the blood around from the buffalo, both my hands were itching and I thought nothing more of it, especially since I was overjoyed with the small piece of meat that had been given to me. I salted and dried it in the sun so that we could save it and eat it a little at a time. However, that night I came down with a fever and Mother gave me the usual medicine which was a drink made from boiled roots. It was bitter, but it brought my fever down.

I kept drinking the medicine for two days and very early on the morning of the third day, the girl from Srae Memai returned. I discovered why she was so keen to persuade me to escape. Apparently the man who had come from the Thai border had been given a special mission – to find me and to help me to escape to Thailand. It was too dangerous for him to come into the middle of Thmar Pouk and so he had sent this girl to find me. He had promised her that he would help her to escape as long as she persuaded me to go with her. This time she had brought a picture which she said was my husband. I took it excitedly and gazed at the picture of a man, a woman and two small girls. Somehow, the woman in the picture looked strangely like me and the man's face was familiar. However, it was definitely not my husband. Disappointed, I told the girl that it was not my husband, but she continued to try and persuade me, saying that the whole village would come too if I only decided to go.

Did the escape of the entire village depend on me? I pondered the situation for a while. I was terrified of being caught by the Khmer Rouge for my supposed collaboration with the Vietnamese, and I had always longed to escape if the opportunity ever presented itself. After all, I reasoned, wasn't it better to risk being robbed in the forest than to face certain death at the hands of the Khmer Rouge? And even if my husband wasn't in Thailand, at least I would be closer in trying to locate him in France. When I explained it like that to myself, it was easy to make the decision. Throwing caution to the winds, I said, "I'll come with you." My mind was made up and the thought of escape now consumed me. I was barely listening as we made arrangements to meet that afternoon at 2 p.m. in Srae Memai.

It would not take long to walk the one kilometre to our rendezvous, so I had the rest of the morning to think about who in my family should come with me on the escape. The excitement of the decision was beginning to wear off and reality was setting in. I thought about the difficulties of escape and the possibility of death. We would have to evade Khmer Rouge patrols, land-mines, booby traps — even wild animals, such as tigers, would be a threat to us. To whom did I have the right to present the option of possible death? How about my children? How would they fare in the depths of the jungle? They might wander off and be lost forever to die a quick and horrible death from wild animals or a slow and agonising death from thirst and starvation. The thought of that possibility happening to either of my precious daughters made me think again about the escape. If I was caught escaping, everyone with me would have been in danger of dying at the hands of the Khmer Rouge. I was the only one who really had no choice but to escape. The small children were in no danger if they stayed with the rest of the family in Thmar Pouk. Besides, I could not imagine myself having the strength to carry Panita and to lead Somaly all the way through the forest to the Thai border. It would be better to split the children and leave one behind so that at least one would survive. Somaly was older – almost ten now – and therefore better able to fend for herself. I could leave Panita with Mother. My thoughts ran on until I came up with a jerk at the realisation of what I was doing. What am I doing? I asked myself. How could I make such a cold-blooded decision to leave one of my children behind? But the mental image of Panita lost in the jungle or with her legs blown off from stepping on a land-mine steeled my heart and I made my decision. I would escape alone with Somaly.

I thought also of my mother, who had been of such great help to me. She had looked after Panita and had taken care of me when I was sick. I could not take her with me. Her blindness precluded that possibility since she would never be able to keep up with the group. It would be difficult for me to leave her behind, but my presence with the family could lead everyone into danger if the Khmer Rouge found me. Besides, I argued with myself, it was not as if I was leaving her alone. My other sisters and brother would take care of her and, anyway, I had no guarantee that I would arrive at the border alive.

I went to see Lay, who had often spoken about escape and told him of my plans. He showed an immediate interest in the possibility of fleeing Cambodia. Mother and Sokhon did not want to be involved in any escape plans, so I decided to ask Da to look after Panita for me. Da agreed immediately and said that I should not worry as she would take good care of Panita. Somaly and I began to get ready, which didn't take long, for we could take very little with us. Just before we left, and as I was wondering how I could say goodbye to Panita, perhaps forever, she ran towards me carrying two tiny cooked fish which Lay had just given to her. They were so small – four centimetres long by one wide – that it was a wonder anyone had been able to catch them. With a sweet smile on her face, she said: "Mummy, I was given two small fish. I'll keep this one for myself and you eat this other one." I looked from the fish up to her large innocent eyes. My heart went out to her and the tears welled up in my eyes. She was only five years old, but she was an important part of my life. How could I possibly leave her behind? I sat down trying to tell myself that I wouldn't regret leaving her. As she came forward into my arms, I could not convince myself. Da could see the emotions playing on my face and could read my mind. She leaned over to me and said quietly: "What would you think about me coming as well? I'll help to take care of Panita on the trail." At the same time, Lay also offered to help with Panita. I felt so grateful to them both and the pain in my heart eased. I would take both my daughters with me and trust God for His protection.

There were about 50 Khmer Rouge camped next to a pond not far from where we lived. We would have to be careful not to arouse their suspicions when we left. We decided to split up. Taking a primitive fishing rod and a small basket with some cooked rice, dried fish and salt, Panita and I walked out of the house as if we were going on a fishing trip. Da and Somaly followed on a different road a little later, carrying another basket and pretending to be going to the fields to collect broken grains of rice.

None of us took any clothes except the ones we were wearing. I had not told my mother that we were leaving as the knowledge of our escape would make it dangerous for her when the Khmer Rouge eventually discovered that we had gone. I was so sad that I did not have the opportunity to say a proper farewell and I hoped that she would find it in her heart to forgive me. My conscience was somewhat eased as I had discussed with her previously the possibility of escaping to the border in the near future.

Arriving in Srae Memai, we found the whole village assembled waiting for us. I was led off into the trees just outside the village to meet the man who had been sent from Thailand to find me. His name was Yom and he was originally from the village of Srae Memai. He held a pistol in his hand and wore black clothing. From his pocket, he extracted a camera and took a photograph of me. After greeting him, I told him that the man in the picture was not my husband and that I was not sure now about escaping. Yom replied that, even if the man was not my husband, I still ought to try to escape from the terror of the Khmer Rouge. I had to agree with what he had said, even though the journey through the forest was going to be hazardous. It was obvious from my discussion with him that he had to make sure that I did escape as he had a mission to accomplish. As I walked back to the village, and saw everyone ready and waiting, I realised that the whole village was getting ready to escape. I found the others waiting for me in a house and we all settled down to wait.

Someone came into the house to tell us that the plan was for us to leave at 6 p.m. that evening. About a dozen ox-carts were going to go first to help carry the elderly people of the village. We were all told that, as soon as we heard the sounds of the ox-carts fading away, we were to follow in groups of four or five. The border was about 35 kilometres away, but we would all assemble at a certain point in the forest about five kilometres outside the village before going on together. All the villagers knew where the meeting point was, so we planned just to follow another group. As we waited for the hour of departure, the air was full of tension. We had mixed emotions of anxiety and fear, but also of excitement. My thoughts drifted to Mother and the rest of my family who were staying behind. What would become of them? I realised that they were probably thinking the same thing about us.

We had been in Srae Memai for only one hour when rumours passed from mouth to mouth; hundreds of Khmer Rouge were pouring into Thmar Pouk; they had already pushed back the Vietnamese; they were going to seize power once more. If they had discovered about the mass escape that was planned from Srae Memai, we would all be caught in a trap. A wave of panic swept over the village as these rumours circulated. Many people were not willing to wait for their assigned time of departure and left right away with some of the ox-carts. In the house where we were sheltering, one person after another left. We had no idea what was going on and wondered what we should do. At 3 p.m. the girl who had come to Thmar Pouk to find me came into the house and told us that half the village had already fled. We had to leave right away. It was 3.30 p.m. as we crept out of the village. There were seven people in our group, and we could see a couple of other groups ahead of us in the forest. We all tried to move slowly, so that if we were spotted by the Khmer Rouge they would think that we were just going into the forest to search for food. However, panic made our feet move faster and we were almost running by the time we arrived at the edge of the forest. Once within the shelter of the trees, we began to feel a little more secure.

A little further on, we finally came across a larger group of villagers. We eagerly joined them and carried on. From not far behind, we heard the sound of ox-carts and running feet. The same thought hit us all simultaneously. It must be the Khmer Rouge chasing us. We ran as fast as we could to try and escape. After a while my lungs heaved with the effort and my legs began to feel as heavy as lead. There was another group ahead of us and they heard our footsteps. They hid in the undergrowth and waited for us. Seeing who we were, they stopped us to ask what was going on. Panita was a little ahead with Da, while Somaly waited with me. I was exhausted and couldn't run any further. We could hear the ox-carts from behind coming closer, but nothing could give me the strength to run more. Our fear gradually began to abate as the leader of the first group explained that there were still a few ox-carts that hadn't arrived yet. We realised with some embarrassment that we had been running away from our own friends, who had probably been rushing to try and catch us up before we disappeared into the forest. It was a great relief to know that we weren't being chased by the Khmer Rouge and, from then on, we were able to walk at a normal pace.

There were altogether just over 200 people, but we still split into smaller groups as we walked. After a while it became a real effort to put one foot in front of the other and my legs ached continuously. Even with the better food which I had enjoyed over the past few weeks, I had still not recovered from the years of virtual starvation. I had no stamina and could only walk slowly. We continued for three hours and then the light began to fade. Yom and three or four men with him moved up and down the line of people giving us encouragement and saying that there wasn't much further to go. Yom had clearly planned the escape for some time and knew exactly what to do. He was clever and well versed in the ways of the Khmer Rouge. Having ox-carts with us meant that any Khmer Rouge we encountered on the way would think that we were a Khmer Rouge convoy heading for sanctuary in the forests close to the border. A few of the villagers had managed to conceal their ox-carts when the Khmer Rouge were confiscating them for their own purposes.

We walked in a long procession split up by all the ox-carts. I watched over Somaly all the time to make sure that she didn't get separated from the main column. Da and Lay were as good as their word and took good care of Panita. Sometimes, Lay carried Panita on his shoulders and sometimes Da gave her a piggyback or held her hand while walking along in the dark. From time to time, Lay lifted Panita up and put her in an ox-cart in spite of the protests from the driver, who feared that the extra weight might break the axle. This gave me an idea and I walked close to an ox-cart with Somaly. I told her to put her hand on to the back of the cart and to hold on tight. This had the effect of dragging her forward. Every two hours or so, Yom let us stop to get about 20 minutes' rest. A half-moon came out and helped us to see our way. It also cast eerie shadows in front of us and made the journey more terrifying as we imagined the Khmer Rouge lying in ambush for us.

At about 9 p.m. Yom's men came down the line and told everyone to stop and not to move. Talking was strictly forbidden and babies were put at their mothers' breasts to prevent them from crying. Silence descended over our group like a blanket and we began to hear the sounds of the jungle which had been previously masked by the noise of the column. From far away, the wind brought us the long drawn-out cry of a wild animal. We had no idea what was going on, but we were frozen in fear. Someone whispered that it was a Khmer Rouge recognition signal. This meant that we had been heard and a Khmer Rouge patrol was trying to check our identity. We were in trouble and I wondered how far we could all run before the Khmer Rouge would catch up with us and begin shooting. I imagined bullets ripping into my flesh and into my children's bodies.

Now the man who had recognised the Khmer Rouge

signal approached Yom and said: "I used to work closely with the Khmer Rouge and I know all of the different recognition signals that they use in the forest. If you like, I can give them the correct reply." Yom immediately answered: "Make the signal. You're our only hope of avoiding an ambush." The man then cupped his hands together and emitted a strange cry. The Khmer Rouge call came once more and again the villager replied. We held our breath in suspense and our hearts beat faster. Would it work? There was silence now from the Khmer Rouge and we waited quietly to see what would happen. Our own eyes tried to pierce the gloom of the forest and our ears strained to hear any movements coming towards us. The slightest noise would have started a panic and we would have fled in all directions. However, after some time there was still no sound from the direction of the cry and we began to have hope that the ploy had succeeded. Yom thanked the villager and we set off once more towards the border.

As we walked, I noticed that the hand which I had nicked with a knife while cutting up the buffalo meat was still itching. However, in my almost permanent state of fear, I paid it little attention.

We were now deep in the middle of the forest and, in the moonlight, we could make out the shape of a building some way ahead. Yom stopped the group and went ahead with one other man to check it out. He found it to be deserted and motioned us all foward. It was an old military base that had been set up by the Lon Nol regime during the civil war. The sight of it in the middle of the forest made us all tremble with fear as we realised that there was a real possibility of the Khmer Rouge being there. However, the Khmer Rouge had not taken it over, but had set up their own base further down the forest trail. The building was in a state of disrepair, with holes in the roof and hardly any walls. On the other side of the track lay the twisted skeleton of a jeep that had been abandoned. We walked past the building and then Yom struck off to one side to avoid the Khmer Rouge base further down the track. Several men led the way and hacked at the undergrowth with machetes to allow the passage of the ox-carts.

As we moved forward shortly before midnight, an ox-cart ahead of us stopped. The yoke for the buffaloes had broken. The two girls who had been in the cart were trying to mend it. Some people stopped to help but, with no tools, repair seemed impossible in the dark. As I approached they asked me to wait for them. I felt sorry for them, so I waited while they tried to fix the yoke themselves. I was sorry that I could do nothing to help them. Somaly kept dragging on my sleeve and urging me to keep going as we had almost lost sight of the group who were now well ahead of us. Finally, I apologised to the girls and we hurried on, trying to catch up with the main body of the group. Panita was with Da and Lay, who were way ahead of us. We kept walking until after midnight, when Yom finally halted the whole group since we seemed to be covering the same ground. In fact we were just walking round and round in circles. Having left the forest trail to avoid the Khmer Rouge, he had become disoriented and we were now lost in the forest.

We sat down to rest while several men climbed tall trees in an attempt to see where we were. The dim light given by the moon made it difficult to identify any landmarks. While we rested, there was a commotion from the back. Some stragglers, including the two girls whose ox-cart had broken, had finally caught up. Most people were talking in low voices and the babies and small children in the group were already crying because of thirst, which only added to the noise. Most of us had used up what little water we had brought with us and we were all beginning to feel weak from the lack of it. Two men went out in widening circles around the group to try and locate a water source. Eventually they found a small pond and several people took the containers which they had brought with them to fill up with water. These were carried back and shared out amongst everyone.

Somaly was very tired and lay on the ground where she had collapsed when we had all stopped. Panita was still sitting on the cart, but she was in tears and very frightened that she might get separated from us. She was also afraid that the cart driver might throw her off his cart. Da stayed close to comfort her. Somaly said that she could not go on any further and that she was going to sleep. She dozed off immediately and I let her sleep. Soon after, everyone started to get up and leave again. No one had said anything, but I guessed that they had finally worked out where we were. I shook Somaly to wake her up. She curled up tighter and mumbled that she was too tired and that she just wanted to sleep. It was time for some shock tactics. I told her that she could sleep, but she would have to stay alone. It was cruel but effective. She scrambled up immediately and we continued on our journey. There was no trail now and we had to force our way through bushes and thick under-growth. Branches snatched at our faces and at our clothes, and left red weals down our cheeks. The trees soared above us and blocked out any light from the stars and the moon. The soles of our feet became scratched and torn and it was acutely painful to walk.

The ground was very uneven and, on a couple of oc-casions, we came to a deep depression. The men searched around in the forest to find bamboo, which they cut down and tied together to make a bridge for the ox-carts. Time seemed to drag on forever. Would we ever find our way out of this forest? I was very tired and my mind started to play tricks on me. The trees looked like men. The branches were AK47 rifles and B40 rocket launchers. Would the night ever end?

At some point in the journey, an elderly woman died

and the column stopped. We were towards the back and didn't know what was going on. A few people screamed. Most of us were too tired to react and we remained where we were. Some ran towards the screams. There was no time to bury the old lady, even though we knew that her body would be eaten by wild animals if we left her. Her family had an ox-cart. They took their possessions off it and gently laid the body of the woman on top of it. This was her coffin and funeral pyre although we could not set fire to it for fear of attracting the Khmer Rouge. The column moved on with the family weeping quietly. My heart went out to the family and I felt for them. While we all knew of the possibility of death on the escape, this was the first one. I wondered how many more would die before we could reach safety.

We knew that we were getting closer to the border and we walked in single file. Yom ordered us not to stray from the path because of land-mines. We came across a cleared area, which was covered with bamboo spikes. They had been dug into the ground by the Khmer Rouge and were specifically designed to prevent people from escaping. They were angled towards us and each one had been sharpened. The Khmer Rouge had painted the tip of each spike with a poison made from boiling a concoction of roots together so that any wound caused by it would fester. The spikes were intended to prevent people from running in the event of their being chased by the Khmer Rouge. At regular intervals there were also holes dug in the ground covered with dried grass and, as I was told, lined with bamboo spikes at the bottom. These were intended to snare the unwary, who would have been impaled on the spikes if they had fallen into the holes. Land-mines had also been planted indiscriminately.

Fortunately, the Khmer Rouge didn't have enough men to patrol all the time, so if we could get through these obstacles safely, we might yet survive. There was ample evidence of those who had tried unsuccessfully to escape before us. As dawn broke, I could see skeletons from afar. Over the whole place of horror lay the smell of rotting flesh. We could not see the decomposing corpses but they were there somewhere – perhaps caught in one of the spiked holes. I shuddered and kept a tight grip on Somaly as we went forward.

On the far side of the area with the bamboo spikes, Yom turned around and announced to everyone that we had just crossed the border out of Cambodia into Thailand. It was about 5 a.m. on Sunday, March 11th, 1979. Relief washed through us all and there was a feeling of joy in the air. We had made it. I hugged Somaly and went to find Panita and Da to give them hugs as well. I thanked Lay and Da for their help with Panita. Without them, my joy would have been empty.

There was no time for a party and we had to get away from the border as soon as possible. We could hear the sound of dogs barking and cocks crowing in the distance. It was a familiar sound to us who had lived in villages for so many years. Then, it had meant the start of another day of slavery under the Khmer Rouge. Now, it signified that we were near a Thai village and freedom. As we walked towards the village, Yom told us to hide our belongings in case of interception by bandits. We walked quietly waiting to see what would happen. We came across a pond with dirty water and everyone stopped to drink because we were so thirsty. At 6 a.m. we reached a tarmac road. It was like moving into a new world after the forest and all the dirt tracks in Cambodia. We didn't know what the future held but, for once, we felt free.

11   . . . Into the Fire

As we walked along the road towards the nearby town of
Ta Phraya, we encountered some Thai soldiers who were
out on patrol. They ordered us to stop and then began to
question us in Thai. One of the villagers, who spoke a little
Thai, came forward. The Thai soldiers seemed kind, but
they wanted to know where we had come from and
whether we were carrying any weapons. Yom was the only
one with a pistol and he had already slipped away. We were
a motley crowd and did not seem to pose any danger to
the soldiers. Most of us only had the clothes on our backs
and were dressed in black or grey clothing – the standard
Khmer Rouge issue for all peasants. As the Thais questioned
the villager, the rest of us sank down on to the edge of the
road, glad at last to be able to rest.

The soldiers were led by a sergeant who was unsure of
what he should do. One of his men had a radio pack on his
back and the sergeant walked over to it. He spoke rapidly
in Thai and seemed to be asking for instructions. We waited
patiently. About two hours later we heard the sound of a
vehicle and an army jeep came into view. As it came to a
halt, an officer jumped out. He fired some more questions
at the villager and then sent some of the patrol off to check
the border area where we had crossed over. The rest of the
soldiers herded us together and indicated that we should
keep walking towards the town of Ta Phraya. As we
reached the boundary of the town, we were ordered to halt
under a large tree. We were allowed to sit down while

waiting, but the shade from the tree was not enough and many of us had to sit in the hot sun until 2 p.m. During the morning a policeman came from the town and began the task of counting us. There were more questions and the police started to make a list of our names. Altogether there were 207 people in our group.

We had had no food now for some time and were beginning to get very hungry. The children, especially, found it difficult. However, no one complained or dared to ask the soldiers and police for food. The Thai villagers knew that we had come from a country where we had been denied proper food, and very kindly offered some to the children and to the elderly among us.

At around 4 p.m., six army trucks pulled up on the road in front of us and we were all ordered to climb on. The next stage in our trek to freedom was about to begin. It felt so good to be free and to be travelling in a vehicle again. It didn't matter that it was just an open-top army truck. To me, it seemed as if it were a Mercedes Benz. I squeezed Somaly and Panita close to me and revelled in this new sense of freedom. My right hand continued to itch but I ignored it, thinking it unimportant.

The road led southwards. It was long and straight, with rice fields off to either side. My knowledge of the geography of Thailand was limited, but I realised that we were travelling parallel to the border and that we were heading towards the town of Aranya Prathet. We travelled for about 50 kilometres and occasionally passed Thai villages off to one side of the road. Towards the end of the journey, we crossed over a railway line and swung left into the town. It was larger than Ta Phraya and there was a sense of bustle to it. We went through the middle and then continued north. We passed over a bridge and saw an enclosed space on our left. Barbed wire was strung all around and there were several hundred people inside. The trucks went to the entrance and the gates were swung open to admit us. As we all climbed down from the trucks, we realised that everyone else in this place was Cambodian. There were about 1,500 who had been there for several weeks already. They came crowding round us to find out who we were and where we had come from. They were also excited to see if there were any of their relatives among us.

In the distance I saw a familiar face and recognised it as the man in the picture that Yom had brought into Cambodia. He looked very much like my cousin, Hay Peng Kry, whom I hadn't seen for more than 15 years. As soon as he approached our group, I realised immediately that he was searching for his wife. So I went forward to greet him and introduced myself to him and told him that it was me whom Yom had guided out of Cambodia. A look of disappointment came over his face. He told me that his name was Hay Peng Sy and gradually the story came out. He had heard a rumour that his wife was in Thmar Pouk and he had sent Yom in to bring her out. By a strange coincidence, the picture of his wife looked remarkably like me and thus the confusion had arisen. Peng Sy had assumed that Yom was leading his wife to freedom. However, he soon cheered up because our long conversation revealed that we were distant relatives and, to find any kind of relative after the killings by the Khmer Rouge, was a success.

I soon discovered that Peng Sy came from a different refugee camp. It was about seven kilometres on the north side of Aranya Prathet and was called Ban Thai Samart. In fact we must have driven right past it without realising it. Peng Sy had come over to this new temporary camp, called Wat Koh, to use his engineering skills in the construction of shelters and toilets. He told me that he was helping a foreigner who had a programme to assist the refugees. As we were talking, Peng Sy took me to an area where several items were being distributed. He arranged for us all to receive plates, spoons, mugs, soap, mats and blankets. I gazed in disbelief at all the different things which we were given. Soap, of all things! I hadn't seen a proper bar of soap since we left Phnom Penh four years previously. We had washed using only water. Now, at last, I might be able to feel clean once again. While the shelters were being built, Peng Sy secured us a place to sleep underneath some trees. We put down our mats and 'claimed' our piece of ground. Food was being cooked in groups and Peng Sy assigned us to a group. It was amazing what he was able to do. All the other refugees looked upon him with a great deal of respect.

In the evening, I looked up from where I was sitting and talking to Peng Sy: a foreigner was walking through the middle of the camp. He was taller than most of the Cambodians and had a black beard. He didn't seem to smile and looked stern from a distance. I nudged Peng Sy and asked him who he was. Peng Sy looked up and saw the man. He broke into a smile and said: "That's Robert. He's the foreigner whom I told you about. He has a programme to help feed the refugees in the other camp and he is also providing the material for shelters, toilets and cooking equipment here. I'll introduce him to you, since you speak English." With that, he jumped up and strode off to meet the foreigner. I wasn't at all sure that I wanted to meet such a stern-looking person, but Peng Sy brought him right over. He greeted me with hands clasped together in the traditional Khmer way. "Hello," he said, "Peng Sy tells me that you speak English." I had forgotten all about my English and now I forced myself to remember the words which I had tried to forget while working under the Khmer Rouge. I began to speak hesitatingly and it started to come back to me. Robert smiled, which broke the hardness of his face and made it easier for me to speak English again. I called over Somaly and Panita to introduce them to Robert. Neither of them could remember seeing a foreigner before and I expected them to be either shy or frightened of such a strange-looking man with hair all over his face. However, they greeted him warmly and seemed to accept him easily. He stayed only a few minutes and then went away with Peng Sy, apparently to discuss the construction of additional shelters and toilets for our new group.

That evening we were able to get a good plate of rice with some meat and vegetables. It was so good to be able to eat good food again, and to have enough of it. With full stomachs, we lay down on our mats. We were all exhausted, but the excitement of being free kept us awake late into the night before we could fall asleep. I woke early the next morning and felt once again that my hand was itching. It was irritating and I scratched it without thinking. Then, looking at it more closely, I saw that there was a little red spot in the place where I had nicked it with the knife. I wondered if there was a little infection inside which was causing the itch. I went to see some of the refugees who had been in Wat Koh for several weeks and asked them if it was possible to get any medical treatment. They told me that the Thai Red Cross came with a team of doctors and nurses each morning and that I would probably be able to get something from them.

Sure enough, at around 10 a.m., a Land-Rover with red crosses on the sides pulled into the camp. The nurses set up a table and a queue of people began to form. I joined the line and waited patiently. An hour later I reached the head of the queue and showed my hand to one of the nurses. She looked at it and, before I could explain anything to her, she picked up a bottle of gentian violet and a piece of cotton wool and dabbed some of it on to my hand. As I started to ask her in English what I should do, she waved me away and started talking to the next patient.

There was little to do except return to our place under the trees. Somaly and Panita seemed happy. They had found other children of their own ages and were playing with them. Da and I helped the group to prepare the midday meal and then we all took our plates to eat under the trees. My hand continued to itch and was slightly swollen and I frequently scratched at it. I noticed that Peng Sy and the foreigner, Robert, were again in the camp organising the construction of new shelters. Towards early evening they began to get ready to leave the camp. Peng Sy and Robert walked over to see us and to say good-bye. They sat down for a few minutes to talk and, after a while, Robert noticed that my hand was swollen. He saw the purple colour from the gentian violet and asked what was the problem. I explained the background and he said that I ought to go back and see the Thai Red Cross again the next day. He was about to get up and go, when he asked to look closer at my hand. I held out my arm. The red spot had now become a little blister. A look of concern flashed across Robert's face. He called Peng Sy to have a look and pointed out that there were tiny red lines running from the blister up my arm. He explained to me that it was an infection and that there was some kind of poison inside my hand which was spreading up my arm.

Taking Peng Sy with him, he went off to talk to the Thai camp commander. After some considerable discussion, they came back. Peng Sy explained to me that Robert had asked permission for me to be taken to the small hospital in the other camp of Ban Thai Samart. The commander had refused but, when Robert insisted, he had finally agreed to allow me to be taken to see an American doctor in Aranya Prathet on condition that I be brought straight back to the camp. I got into the front of Robert's Datsun pick-up truck together with Peng Sy and we drove out of the camp. Robert drove quickly to a small house in the middle of the town and took me inside where I met the American doctor. His name was John Naponnick and he was very kind. Robert explained the problem and the doctor gently took my arm to examine my hand. Without doing tests, he could not be sure what it was, but he knew that it was something serious. He recommended to Robert that I be taken to the hospital in Ban Thai Samart camp and be put on a heavy dose of penicillin. This put Robert in a quandary as he had promised the Wat Koh commander to take me straight back. I was in a daze by now, wondering what was going on and what strange disease I had caught. My hand was giving me considerable pain and I wanted desperately to go to the hospital and get some medicine.

Robert thought about the problem for a while and then decided to take me to the hospital. I think he felt that he could explain the reasons to the Thai camp commander later on. I followed meekly back to the car and we all got in. I asked Peng Sy what it was all about and he calmed me down by assuring me that everything was all right. We reached the other camp within 15 minutes and the Thai guards opened the gates for Robert's vehicle without any questions. He drove immediately to the hospital. I noticed that John Naponnick's car was right behind. John swung quickly into action and arranged a bed for me. In the meantime, he opened the medicine cabinet and took out the penicillin. I flinched as the needle went in. I hated injections and couldn't stand the sight of blood. I asked Peng Sy if he could go back to Wat Koh to check on Somaly and Panita and to reassure them. He said that he would, and I watched him and Robert walk away.

The next morning I lay back on the hospital bed and tried to relax. It was difficult, as my thoughts constantly turned towards my children and Da and Lay. I wished they were here with me. I felt alone and wondered again what the future held. My arm was hurting more and more. I looked at it and could see that the red lines had reached even further. There was a throbbing pain and it hurt me to move it. That night I was unable to sleep for even a minute. As the hours dragged by, my entire right arm throbbed painfully and I was barely able to stop myself screaming with the pain.

I thought finally of God. He had provided for my every need so far and had brought me safely into Thailand. "Lord, don't leave me now," I prayed. "I'm alone, without family, in this hospital and I need You more than ever." A sense of peace stole over me and I slipped into an uneasy broken sleep.

In the morning, I awoke to find my arm hugely swollen and throbbing intensely. The back of my right hand was completely red and the blister had grown in size. I began to be afraid. What was happening to me? The American doctor, John, arrived at 8.30 a.m. and his presence comforted me. He examined me once more and then gave me more penicillin. He explained that he still didn't know what it was, but he was increasing the penicillin dose to combat the poison. As the day wore on, I became feverish. The Khmer medical orderlies kept coming in to sponge me down to try and bring down my temperature, but to no avail. By the evening, I was delirious. For the next three days I remained largely unconscious, knowing almost nothing of what was happening. From time to time I came out of my delirium and found myself weeping with pain, but mercifully slipped back into oblivion after only a few minutes.

Peng Sy managed to persuade the local district officer, who was in charge of both camps, to allow Somaly and Panita to come to Ban Thai Samart camp to be with me. He took care of them in his own home. Although they came to visit me in the hospital, I was unaware of their presence. The results from the blood tests came back and showed that I had anthrax. No one knew much about it, but it is a cattle disease that can also affect humans. It seemed that the buffalo in Thmar Pouk had died from anthrax. When I had assisted in cutting up the carcass, the anthrax organism had entered into my bloodstream through the little nick from the knife. It had incubated for the next few days while I made my escape. If I had delayed my escape by one or two days, I would have died. God's timing is truly wonderful!

As soon as anthrax was diagnosed, there was fear that others might be contaminated. There were no isolation facilities in the camp and so I was transferred, unconscious, to the Thai District Hospital in Aranya Prathet. I was placed on a bed in a small room. Somehow, Da was able to find a way to slip out of Wat Koh camp and to come to the hospital to help take care of me. Da stood or sat next to my bed all the time. At night, she lay down on a mat on the floor. She bathed my forehead as I sweated out the fever. After two days I regained consciousness. Looking up from my supine position, I saw Da leaning over me. I looked slowly round the room. "Where am I?" I whispered. Da comforted me and explained what had been taking place.

My thoughts turned to my children, "What about Somaly and Panita?" Again Da reassured me that they were safe. I relaxed on the bed and leaned over to look at my right hand. I was horrified by what I saw. My arm was even more swollen than before I had slipped into unconsciousness. That I had expected, but what shocked me was the sight of huge water blisters, some as big as tennis balls, hanging from my right arm. My hand was covered with a bandage and so I could not see what had become of the small blister. The arm itself was a nasty red and purple colour. An intravenous tube hung down from the other side of the bed and liquid flowed into my left arm through a needle. Looking at my arm, I began to wonder if I was going to survive or not. Perhaps death awaited me at the end of this awful experience. At this thought, tears welled up in my eyes and began to stream down my face.

A day or so later, a Thai man in a white coat walked in through the door. He introduced himself in English and said that he was the doctor who was in charge of my case. He sat down on the edge of the bed and gently unwound the bandage from my hand. I had been shocked at the sight of my arm, but I gazed at my hand with a feeling of revulsion. The little blister had gone. It had been replaced by a mass of rotting flesh on my swollen hand. An area of skin of almost two inches diameter was gone. In the middle of the infected area I could see the bones of my hand surrounded by greyish, dead flesh. The doctor looked at me and said: "You have contracted a very serious disease which is usually fatal. The penicillin given to you by the American doctor has probably saved your life. However, the poison from the infection is still spreading into your body and it could still prove fatal unless I operate right away." I was not at all sure what he was talking about and I asked him, "What do you mean – operate?" His reply left me speechless. "I am sorry, but I must amputate your arm to prevent the infection spreading further. It is the only thing that can save your life."

"I would rather die than lose my arm," I blurted out. I looked over at Da beseechingly, but she could only stare helplessly. The doctor slowly bandaged up my hand and said, "It's your choice, but you must be aware of the consequences if you do not let me operate." With that he left the room. In the afternoon the American doctor, John, came in to see me and I told him what the Thai doctor had said. He told me: "In serious cases like this, often the only way to save the patient's life is to amputate. However, I think Robert brought you to me early enough for the penicillin to fight the infection. I think it is worth waiting a couple more days to see how you progress." I breathed a sigh of relief at this ray of hope now presented to me. Over the next two days, I watched my arm carefully and I spent much time in prayer. Surely God would not desert me now. Little by little, the terrible throbbing in my arm stopped. Although the awful purple colour and the blisters remained, I knew that my arm was saved and I thanked God. Robert came in to see me on a couple of occasions and each time he brought Somaly and Panita with him. I was overjoyed to see them again and they both seemed happy and well. They obviously got on well with Robert even though communication was restricted to smiles and waves.

After a few days, the Thai doctor came to see me again and said that he was glad to see that my arm was getting better and that it would not need amputation. He said that I was well enough to go back to the little hospital in the Ban Thai Samart refugee camp. Robert came in that afternoon and took Da and me back to the camp. I went into the camp hospital to see John. He examined my arm once more and said that I didn't need to stay in the hospital if I didn't want to. Peng Sy was there and he told me that Da and I could go and stay in a small house with Somaly and Panita close to his home. John told me that I would have to come to the hospital each day to have my hand washed and the bandage changed. The awful blisters gradually disappeared and the colour of my arm returned to normal. What did not go away was the hole in the back of my swollen hand. John kept treating it, hoping that as the blood flowed back, some of the cells would come alive again. It was not to be. Eventually, he had to cut away a lot of dead flesh. This was an agonising experience. Each morning, I screamed with pain as a nurse scraped my hand trying to remove the rotten flesh and clean the wound. This went on for about three weeks before the hole in my hand was gradually covered up with scar tissue.

Life became a routine. The children were happy and their bright smiles caused them to be loved by all in the camp. They had been constricted under the Khmer Rouge and now their real spirits were being released. Once more we all began to hope for the future. Peng Sy took me through the camp to introduce me to different people. One of his best friends was a man called Sarun, who had been a helicopter pilot in Cambodia before the fall of Phnom Penh.

Sarun had also trained at agricultural university and now, together with Peng Sy, ran what was known as the Technical Centre in the camp. There were large numbers of refugees who came to study and train at the Centre. Several Khmer teachers taught subjects such as car repairs, radio repair, metal forge-work, sewing/tailoring and carpentry. Sarun spoke fluent Thai and often acted as the refugees' spokesman in the camp.

Robert often came into the camp to supervise the work of his organisation. He had several people working for him and they conducted a supplementary feeding programme for children who were malnourished. Occasionally he was accompanied by other people who worked in other parts of Thailand. Once he introduced me to a friend called Jeremy, who had worked in Thai villages for many years. He was making his first visit to a refugee camp and he was eager to become involved in the work. Robert told him that he might have some work for him to do later.

Towards the end of March, a television team came out from England to do a story on the new influx of refugees from Cambodia. They filmed the people in Wat Koh, but also came into the Ban Thai Samart camp to do an interview with me. Since I spoke some English, it was easier for them to ask me questions about life in Cambodia. Strictly speaking, I should not have stayed in Ban Thai Samart camp, as I was in a different category of refugees. Now that the Vietnamese were in control of Cambodia and the tight control imposed by the Khmer Rouge was no longer there, the Thais were afraid of a mass influx of refugees from Cambodia. They had made a new rule, saying that anybody who crossed the border into Thailand after January 1st, 1979 would not be considered as a refugee, but would be liable to be returned to Cambodia. This meant that the group of 1,700 in Wat Koh were in potential danger of being sent back. I was not eager to return to Wat Koh, and I was fortunate in that the need for medical attention enabled me to stay in Ban Thai Samart camp.

At 7 a.m. on Thursday, April 12th, 1979, the blow fell. Thai army units led by several intelligence agents arrived at Wat Koh camp with a large number of buses. Lay and the refugees, most of whom were women and children and many of whom had husbands and fathers in the Ban Thai Samart camp, were told that they were being taken to another refugee camp in Klong Yai District. This was in the province of Trat further to the south. It all sounded fairly plausible since everyone knew that 1,200 refugees had been taken to that camp from Wat Koh only two months before. Everyone was quickly bundled on to the buses in seemingly needless haste. The district officer was called and he looked on helplessly. Meanwhile, an army truck was sent off to the Ban Thai Samart camp. In the hospital there were several refugees from Wat Koh, who were either suffering from malaria or tuberculosis. The guards had orders to round up everyone from Wat Koh, whether they were in a fit condition to travel or not. They were taken out of the hospital on stretchers and laid on the floor of the truck. Meanwhile Da, Somaly, Panita and I were staying in the house that Peng Sy had provided for us. I was supposed to return to the hospital each morning to have my bandage changed. That morning, through the grace of God, I was late in setting off for the hospital and so I escaped the net. The truck roared off back to Wat Koh and the buses moved off to the south shortly afterwards. Although assurances had been given by the Thai authorities that preparations had already been made at the other camp in the south, the buses never arrived there. About ten days later, a batch of letters was received in camp. They were written by the people who had been taken out from Wat Koh camp and somehow mailed to their relatives in Ban Thai Samart camp. The letters told the sad story of what had happened. About 20 kilometres north of the city of

Trat, the buses with their military escort had turned off the main road and travelled along a dirt track eastwards. Stopping close to the border, the refugees had been handed over to a group of armed Khmer soldiers who had led them off into the mountains of Cambodia.

We remained in the camp and tried to stay hidden, for we were afraid of being sent back as well. This was difficult to do, for Somaly and Panita were always running around the camp and they were well known with their happy faces. On Tuesday, April 17th, the fourth anniversary of the fall of Phnom Penh to the Khmer Rouge, Robert came into the camp and I went to talk with him. We talked about the situation and I asked him if it was possible for him to get permission for us to go to England. I was too afraid to stay longer in the camp, and I dreaded the thought of being sent back into Cambodia, especially after hearing about what had become of our other friends who had been forced back across the border. Peng Sy was also worried about me, for he knew that we were considered as 'illegals' in the camp. He talked the matter over with Robert and they decided that the best thing would be for Peng Sy to write a letter to the district officer explaining why we were still in the camp. Robert went off to see John Naponnick, who likewise agreed to write a letter saying that I was still in need of medical attention. We knew that the district officer was well aware of our presence in the camp and we were afraid that he might launch a search for us. Robert took the two letters to the district officer, who was a kind man, and he agreed that we should stay where we were for the time being.

From then on we all talked about nothing except how we were going to get out of Thailand. The normal routes of departure as refugees were barred to us, since we were illegals and were not registered in the camp. Representatives from both the French and American embassies came to interview us and said that we would be offered entry visas to their countries. However, when I asked them how they could get us out of the camp and into Bangkok for processing, they were stuck for an answer. Each country had a fairly large resettlement programme and they could only add us to their regular list of people to be moved. However, when the bus came to collect us with other people on the list, we would have been prevented from leaving since our names were not registered with the Thai authorities as being refugees. It seemed that there was no way out.

In the meantime Robert, who worked for an English relief organisation, had been looking into the possibility of obtaining visas for us to go to England. His feeling was that, since Britain did not have a regular resettlement programme, it would be easier to get us through the emigration formalities to leave Thailand. The first task was to get us entry visas for England. His father, Pat Ashe, was a clergyman in England and was well connected. He had been involved in assisting refugees and other needy people in various countries for many years. Now he got in touch with the Home Office and presented our cases on 'compassionate' grounds. He was received with a sympathetic ear, but there were certain procedures to be followed. The applications had to be made through the British Embassy in Bangkok. On May 7th Robert duly submitted the applications there together with some passport-size photos of us all which he had taken.

Meanwhile, we were still living at the camp in fear of our lives. We knew that many refugees there had been in the camp for years and that it could take a long time for the visas to be granted. On May 9th we heard rumours that other newly-arrived refugees, being held in Wat Koh camp and in Ta Phraya police station, were about to be sent back to Cambodia. We were afraid that we might be rounded up as well and so we took the precaution of sneaking out of the camp and into the town of Aranya

Prathet where we hid near the market. We stayed there until late afternoon, when one of the other refugees came in to find us and to tell us that it was a false alarm. We breathed a sigh of relief and returned to the camp, but we were under constant tension and afraid that we might be picked up at any time.

On Friday, May 11th, a new development took place. Julian Manyon, the interviewer from Thames Television, who had been involved in filming the group of 1,700 people at Wat Koh shortly after we had escaped, had heard about them all being sent back. He phoned Robert to ask if there was anything that they could do to help. Robert suggested that they put pressure on the Home Office to grant entry visas for Da and myself and the children. Since we were the only ones left of those who had been forcibly repatriated, Robert was anxious to ensure that we, at least, could leave Thailand for a destination of our own choice. Robert told Julian about the general situation and Julian said that he would call back after they had discussed things amongst themselves. Within an hour he called back to say that the whole film crew was coming back out and would try to get there as soon as possible. They wanted to do another film about the forced repatriation of the 1,700 refugees and another interview with me.

Robert came into the camp on Saturday morning to tell me about it and to say that he thought the film crew would be here on Monday. I think, however, that even Robert was surprised to see Julian standing on his doorstep in Aranya Prathet at 3 p.m. that same afternoon! He told us later that they had caught the Concorde from London to Singapore and had then got a connecting flight to Bangkok. They had not checked into a hotel but had driven straight to Aranya Prathet. After the slow-moving ways of Cambodia the speed of the modern world almost overwhelmed me. The best news that Julian brought was that he had contacted the Home Office just before leaving England and they had assured him that authorisation for the visas would be sent to the British Embassy very soon.

Sunday, May 13th, was a memorable day. Not only was I interviewed by Julian Manyon and his TV crew, during which I was able to explain my fear of being sent back to Cambodia, but it was also the day when Kurt Waldheim, the then Secretary-General of the United Nations, was brought to the camp to see the refugee situation for himself. Sarun, the leader of the Khmers in the camp, gave a welcoming speech to Kurt Waldheim. In his speech he also referred to the group of 1,700 people who had been sent back to Cambodia. Staring through the walls of the building where the speeches were being made were dozens of refugees whose relatives had been among the 1,700. In a dramatic gesture, Sarun pointed to them and pleaded with Kurt Waldheim to ask resettlement countries to open their doors before more Khmer refugees were sent back to probable death in Cambodia. The Secretary-General was visibly shocked by what he was hearing and promised to take up the matter with the Prime Minister of Thailand, whom he was meeting that evening.

Watching from behind a drawn curtain, I was afraid for Sarun because the Thai officials were very angry about the revelations he was making to the Secretary-General. However, Panita, only five years old, had no such fear. As Kurt Waldheim left the building, she ducked underneath the arms of the watchful security guards and ran up to him. She took his hand in hers and walked alongside him. He was clearly delighted at this unexpected display of friendship and it helped to relieve the tension in the camp. Bending down, he gathered Panita in his arms and lifted her up to give her a hug. She then walked with him all the way to the front of the camp where she waved good-bye to him as he was driven away. I could hardly believe that my daughter was brave enough to do such a thing.

The following morning, Robert brought several copies

of different Thai newspapers into the camp. There, on the front page, were a number of pictures of Panita either hand in hand with Kurt Waldheim or hugging him. I called to Panita and she came running over. Showing her the pictures, I asked her: "Why did you go and hold that important man's hand?"

"Oh, him," she replied. "We've been friends for a long time." With that casual remark she ran off to play with some friends. I could only gaze after her, thinking how wonderful childish innocence could be!

The next morning, Monday, May 14th, Robert drove into the camp. "The visas have come through to the British Embassy in Bangkok," he shouted excitedly. My heart gave a leap for joy. I could hardly believe my ears and tears of joy rolled down my cheeks.

12   Flight to Freedom

We had been granted entry visas for Britain. I could almost imagine myself there already. I had never visited Britain before, but I had studied about England while I was learning English in Phnom Penh. I had studied not only the language but also the culture, the way of life and some English literature. Now I was looking forward to seeing those great tourist attractions – Big Ben, the Houses of Parliament, Tower Bridge, the Tower of London, Buckingham Palace and so many more.

But the days dragged by and there seemed to be no movement. I knew that Robert was doing his best to obtain permission for us to leave the camp, but he didn't tell us much about what was going on. In the meantime, the news that I had dreaded came from the International Committee of the Red Cross. Soon after my arrival in Thailand, I had made an enquiry with them to try to trace my husband, Lach Virak Phong, who – I hoped – was still in Paris. As the weeks went by with no news, I had begun to fear the worst. The ICRC had eventually traced Virak Phong's nephew, who was living in Paris. The only news that he was able to provide was that Virak Phong had returned to Cambodia in early 1976. I wrote letters to his nephew, So Bun Theun, to try to find out some more details. The news that I received back desolated me.

Soon after the Khmer Rouge take-over, Virak Phong tried to find out news through some of their people in Paris. He was desperate to meet us again and was willing to try anything. He talked with the Khmer Rouge representative in France, who added his name to a long list of other Cambodians trying to locate their families. Finally, in early 1976, the Khmer Rouge representative arranged a plane to take them all from Paris to Peking and from there to Phnom Penh. He assured all the Cambodians that they would be welcomed with great joy in Cambodia, that their families were being collected to meet them at the airport and that the Angkar needed their help in rebuilding the country. It was not many who had the courage or wisdom to resist such words. Virak Phong was blinded by his love for me and for Somaly and Panita. He climbed aboard the plane and took off into the unknown in the expectation of meeting up with us once more. The truth was cruelly different; but, even then, I was not to find out what had really happened to him for another two years.

Shuttling between Bangkok and Aranya Prathet, Robert continued his efforts to get us to England. He often came into the camp to see us and to fill us in on the latest news. Both Somaly and Panita loved him and would often follow him around the camp. Panita loved being carried by him and sometimes he would pick them both up – one in each arm. As with many of the older men in the camp, they called him 'Bhou', which translates into English as 'Uncle'. Since there were several people whom they called 'Bhou', they needed another word to distinguish him from them. So they took the second syllable of Robert, 'bert', and pronounced it 'Bear', since they had heard most people call Robert, 'Ro-bear', in the French way. 'Bhou Bert' means 'Uncle Bert', but it sounded very much like 'Pooh Bear', from 'Winnie the Pooh'. However, Robert didn't seem to mind his new nickname and responded to 'Bhou Bear' quite naturally with a wide smile.

Robert came into the camp on Wednesday, May 16th. He told me that plans were progressing reasonably well and that he hoped everything would work out. However, as he explained all the details, I began to realise that getting the entry visas to Britain had been the easy part. Getting out of Thailand was going to be much more difficult. He had already been to the British Embassy in Bangkok and they would issue us with identity documents and entry visas without any problem. He had checked with UNHCR (the United Nations High Commissioner for Refugees) and with ICM (the Inter-governmental Committee for Migration), which arranges the air flights for all refugees, and we were tentatively booked on a flight leaving Bangkok for London on Thursday, May 24th. I gulped. That was only a week from tomorrow and we were still illegal refugees in a camp 300 kilometres from Bangkok. I could not imagine how he was going to arrange it.

Robert, himself, conceded that things looked a little bleak. He couldn't just load us into the back of his pick-up truck and drive to Bangkok, because the Thai authorities would not give permission for illegal refugees to be transported to Bangkok. There were several checkpoints along the road to prevent the illegal passage of goods and people. On the bright side, he wasn't too concerned about things if we could get to Bangkok. He planned to surrender us to the Thai Immigration Division there, so that we could be tried as illegal entrants. I gasped as I heard this piece of news. What was he trying to do? Surely the idea was to get us out of Thailand and not to surrender us to the Immigration Police to be sent back across the border to our own country. Robert patiently explained that the Immigration Division in Bangkok would not react in the same way as the Immigration Police stationed close to the border. If we were caught outside of the camp, which was close to the border, then we would simply be sent straight back to Cambodia. However, if we were found in Bangkok, we would be tried as illegal entrants and then deported. Since Robert would have entry visas and tickets for Britain, he would ask for us to be deported to Britain. It was an ingenious idea, but we had 300 kilometres to cover before it could be put into effect.

Robert left again for Bangkok on Friday, May 18th, as he had other work to take care of. He said that he was going to be busy for the next few days, but that he would send his friend, Jeremy, whom he had introduced to us some weeks earlier, to continue working on different options on how to get us to Bangkok. Jeremy arrived in the camp on Sunday afternoon and came to find us and greet us once more. He knew that time was getting short, but he was obviously working on a plan to get us to Bangkok. From our short discussion together, I could tell that he knew many things about the camp and about Thailand and that he had been well briefed on the situation. He had some discussions with Sarun and then left to stay the night in Aranya Prathet. Monday morning arrived and it wasn't until Jeremy came into the camp at around 8.30 a.m. that I realised that this was to be our last day in the camp.

Jeremy called Sarun, Peng Sy, Da and myself together to discuss his plan. "The road to Bangkok is cluttered with checkpoints, which makes it much too risky to try getting you to Bangkok that way. However, we have seats booked for you on a plane leaving Bangkok on Thursday night. That means we have four days to get you to Bangkok, process your papers through the Embassy and ICM and also to take you to the Immigration Division. We have just about enough time, but we have to move fast. You will have to take the train to Bangkok because I suspect that there are no identity checks. A friend of mine left at 5.30 this morning on a train to Bangkok. She is going to call me after she arrives to let me know what the security is like. If there are no checks, then you go tomorrow morning at the same time."

My mind was in a spin. Tomorrow morning! I didn't have too many things to pack, so that wasn't a problem, but I had a host of other unanswered questions. How were we supposed to buy the train tickets, since we didn't speak Thai? How would we know when to get off the train? The whole prospect of travelling alone on the train appalled me. I knew I would look so guilty that someone would be bound to ask me questions.

Jeremy interrupted my thoughts by answering the very questions in my mind. "We will need someone, who speaks fluent Thai, to accompany you." Turning to Sarun, he asked: "Sarun, your Thai is excellent. Would you be willing to go with them on the train?" Sarun didn't hesitate. "Of course," he replied, "you can count on me." Jeremy smiled with satisfaction. That was obviously one hurdle over.

"Good, thank you. Now, we need one other person. You see," Jeremy went on to explain, "it will be too obvious if there is only one man with two women and two children. We need to split you up into two groups. One man, one woman and one child. You'll be much less conspicuous that way and I think you'll get through without any problems."

It was hard enough to think of one refugee whose Thai was fluent enough to make people think that he was Thai himself, but to come up with two people was surely asking too much. However, Jeremy seemed to have someone in mind already. He then addressed Sarun: "Sambat, who teaches English in the camp, is just the person we need. Sarun, let's go together and ask him." They both disappeared and came back 15 minutes later together with Sambat, who had a big grin all over his face. It was clear that Sambat was looking forward to the trip to Bangkok.

Jeremy continued to outline his plans. "Sarun, you should escort Da and Somaly. You cannot speak Khmer to each other, so if you have to say anything to Da, you can say it in French, since both of you speak French. Sambat, you accompany Var and Panita and, if necessary, you can both speak in English. Remember, never speak in Khmer or you'll give yourselves away."

That was easy to say, but I knew there would be a hundred and one reasons why Somaly and Panita would want to ask questions during the journey and the only language they spoke was Khmer. I put the problem to Jeremy, but he already had the answer. "I'm going to get some sleeping tablets from the hospital. You must give half a tablet to Somaly and a quarter of a tablet to Panita. That should make them drowsy enough to sleep for the whole journey, especially if you keep them up late tonight." I began to relax a little as all my questions were answered, but I knew that I would sleep very little that night in anticipation of what tomorrow would bring. Jeremy finished by saying, "I have to go back to Aranya Prathet now to wait for a call from Bangkok. As soon as I get the answer from my friend about the checks on the train, I'll come back and let you know. I'll also want to collect your bags, because I can take those with me in the car when I drive to Bangkok." With that he was gone and we had the rest of the day to wait.

Shortly after 5 o'clock that afternoon, Jeremy came back into the camp. He gathered us together and, with a big smile said: "It worked. There are no checks on the train. That means that you all leave tomorrow morning." I think I had only half believed it before; now it began to hit home. We were about to leave! I looked over at Da and we smiled at each other. Jeremy carried on: "Now, before you go rushing out to say good-bye to all your friends in the camp, remember that there are informants in the camp. You must go to sleep quite normally tonight. If you tell anyone, then it's quite likely that the Thais will come to arrest you tonight or they will be waiting for you tomorrow. You mustn't even tell the children. Simply wake them up tomorrow morning and tell them you're leaving. Go out through the side of the camp and meet me 300 metres down the road. I'll be waiting for you all at 4.45 a.m."

Jeremy quietly collected a few small bags of our

belongings and loaded them into the back of his vehicle. Before leaving, he said to me: "When you pray tonight, ask God to provide a heavy rainfall tomorrow morning, so that the guards stay in their huts. That way, your exit will be less noticeable." With that he drove off and we were left to our thoughts.

It was difficult to act normally. I was both excited and afraid. Excited, because here, at last, was the opportunity to begin a new life. Afraid, because something might go wrong and we might end up back amongst the killing inside Cambodia. I prayed quietly to myself: "Lord, grant us your protection in the days ahead and give me the words to speak whenever I am questioned." Somaly and Panita came running up. They had been away playing with some friends. "Where's Pooh Bear?" they demanded. They were hoping that he had come back from Bangkok as they wanted to have a ride in his vehicle, which was such a novelty to them after Cambodia.

"He hasn't come back yet, but you should get a ride in a car tomorrow," I replied. Satisfied, they scampered off to play again. The evening passed by slowly. We cooked our rice and I carefully gathered together the few things which we would have to carry with us the next day. Peng Sy kept talking to, and playing with, Somaly and Panita. Their eyelids were starting to droop, but he managed to keep them awake until 10.30 p.m. Finally they lay down and were asleep within seconds. The rest of us made our way to our beds. Tomorrow would be a long day and we would need as much rest tonight as we could get. Sarun set his alarm clock and promised to wake us up at 4 a.m.

I lay down and prayed to God that He would provide rain to cover our escape out of the camp. Then I tried to sleep. My mind dwelt on what might happen the next day. All sorts of scenarios were conjured up in my mind and each one led to our capture and forced repatriation across the border. When, at last, I fell into a troubled sleep, it was to see the evil faces of the Khmer Rouge leering at me and telling me in detail how they were going to kill me for having deserted the Angkar. They raised their guns to fire and I cowered backwards.

I awoke to hear a heavy roll of thunder. Outside, it was pouring with rain. There were flashes of lightning followed by more thunder. The rain came down in torrents and the roof, made only from grass thatch, soon started to leak. It was not going to be possible to go back to sleep in this! I looked over at Somaly and Panita. They were dead to the world and oblivious to the thunder. I found a small sheet of plastic and covered them up so that they would not get wet from the leaking roof. The rains were early this year, especially such heavy rains. Normally they didn't start until around the middle of June. This seemed like a miracle – the Lord had answered our prayers and had arranged the rain specially to shield our exit from the camp. No one would be out in such a downpour, and even the Thai guards would be safely in their guard huts instead of out on patrol.

Da was already awake and we talked quietly about the coming day. It was not long before Sarun and Sambat came to see if we were awake. We decided that it would be best for us to make our escape while there was still heavy rain. Da and I shook the girls awake. They were both still groggy with sleep and not really aware of what was happening. I got some water and carefully broke a sleeping tablet in half. I gave one half to Somaly. She made a face as she swallowed her medicine, but was too sleepy to argue. Then I took the other half and broke it again to give a quarter to Panita. She, too, swallowed it without protest and then we were ready to leave.

Sarun led the way to a point at the fence which was midway between two guard huts. We trailed behind, trying to cover our heads with pieces of plastic. Peng Sy carried Panita while Sarun and Sambat guided us and watched carefully to make sure that we were not being observed. I pulled Somaly along by her hand to prevent her from lying down and going to sleep again. Distant flashes of lightning illuminated our path from time to time. There were no shouts or warning shots as we ducked underneath the strands of barbed wire. On the other side there was a rice field and the rain had already turned it to mud. We squelched through it and were unable to prevent ourselves from falling over and becoming partly covered with mud. Eventually we reached the road. Turning left, we continued walking to put a safe distance between ourselves and the camp entrance. We disturbed two dogs on the way and they set up a loud howling. I was very afraid that they might wake the villagers, which would have been dangerous for us. It seemed a lifetime before they finally quietened down. When we were several hundred metres from the camp, we moved back from the road and hid ourselves among the trees by the side. The rain had almost stopped now and we could only wait.

At almost exactly 4.45 a.m. we saw the headlights of a vehicle in the distance. The car approached slowly and Sarun whispered: "Stay here." He got up and walked out to the side of the road. The car swung round in a half circle, briefly lighting us up in its headlights. Jeremy stuck his head out of the window: "Hello. I hope you haven't been waiting long." It was a relief to see his smiling face and we moved quickly to climb into the back of the car. There was no time to lose as we didn't want to be seen climbing into a vehicle at this hour of the morning. Our feet left mud all over the place, but there was nothing we could do about it. Sarun and Sambat squeezed into the front of the car and we waved good-bye to Peng Sy as Jeremy drove off with us towards Aranya Prathet. It was about seven kilometres and we would actually cross the railway line before coming to the station. However, Jeremy stopped the car 100 metres from the railway line and turned round to speak to us in the back of the car. "It's best if you walk from here. If the

Thais see a foreigner dropping off several people, they'll be suspicious," he explained.

Turning to Sarun, he said: "Here's money for the train tickets and for you to get something to eat along the way. The railway station is only 200 metres down the track. It would be best if you leave the others in the shadows while you buy the tickets on your own. Then all get on the train at the last minute. When you come into Bangkok, get off at Makasarn Station. It's the one before the main Bangkok Station. If there is any checking, it will be done at the main station. If you get off at Makasarn, you'll be fine and you can take a taxi to Robert's house from there. Robert will probably be there writing letters and will be very surprised to see you. However, he'll know what to do with you after that."

Jeremy shook hands with both Sarun and Sambat. He clasped each one by the shoulder and thanked them. Then turning to us all, he said: "God bless you all. I hope you have a safe journey to Bangkok." We thanked Jeremy for his help and waved to him as he drove away. In the short time that we had known him, he had proved to be a good friend.

There was a hint of dawn in the sky and we walked quickly towards the station. The train was already there. Sarun bought the tickets and came back to join us. It would leave soon, so we decided to get on and find a seat. There were not too many people yet, so we quickly found seats. Although we moved in two separate groups, we sat fairly close to provide moral support for each other. Panita, always a lively girl, was beginning to wake up. "Oh, help," I thought, "the sleeping pill wasn't enough. If she talks in Khmer, she'll give us away." I whispered very quietly to Panita that she was not to say anything. Then I took out of my pocket the other quarter of the sleeping pill and gave it to her. She swallowed it and sat back. The train started up soon afterwards and the swaying motion soon rocked Panita to sleep.

The train moved very slowly. Jeremy had said that it would take about six hours to reach Bangkok. I wondered how we would feel at the end of the journey. It wasn't long before I began to doze off. I had not had much sleep during the night and now I was sleepy. I was jerked awake as the train carriages bumped to a halt at the town of Wattana Nakhon. Peering out through the window, I could see a fairly large crowd of people waiting to get on. Many of them had boxes and bags and were probably going to a larger market nearby to sell their goods. I settled back on the wooden seat, grateful that we at least had somewhere to sit down. With all these new people, some would have to stand.

Out of the corner of my eye, I saw a flash of khaki uniform. I made a sign to Sarun and he also spotted what I was looking at. Coming through the doorway were several Thai policemen. I froze in my seat and wondered if we were about to experience an identity check. The policemen talked easily amongst themselves and made their way down the aisle towards us. I glanced at Somaly and Panita, made sure that they were asleep and then closed my eyes. I heard the policemen come closer to us and then they stopped. My heart was beating faster and faster and my mind wondered what they were doing. If they looked closely at me, they would surely see me trembling. I forced myself to relax my eyelids. Their conversation started up again and they moved on. I breathed a sigh of relief keeping my eyes shut. This was indeed going to be a long journey.

There were stops at several smaller stations and then we arrived at Kabinburi, where finally the policemen and many other passengers disembarked. From then on, the journey seemed to be easier. We passed between forests and hills on the one side and rice paddy-fields on the other. There were many water buffaloes in the fields and sometimes we passed people working in the fields, either preparing the ground for the next planting or finishing the harvest of the dry-season crop. If it wasn't for the tension that we were under, it would have been a lovely way to have seen Thailand.

After about four hours, we arrived in the town of Chachoengsao. Sarun bought a little food and something to drink from the vendors who came to the train windows to sell their wares in baskets. The children slept on and we didn't disturb them. They could eat and drink later when we were out of danger. There was a whistle and the train lurched as we set off once more. Now the countryside was beginning to change. There were large expanses of rice fields on both sides and the land was completely flat. We could often see clusters of houses and even some factories from time to time. Then, away in the distance, we began to see the build-up of houses and taller buildings. We had reached Bangkok – but we were not yet safe.

Even as we came into the city, there were still many stops at small stations along the way. Sarun asked someone where Makasarn Station was and he was told that it was still some way ahead. As the train drew to a halt at yet one more place, a man next to Sarun nudged him and told him that this was Makasarn. Both Somaly and Panita were beginning to stretch, so it didn't take long to wake them up. Silencing their very obvious questions, we all scrambled up and made for the doorway. There were others descending as well and we had plenty of time. We climbed down by the railway tracks and Sarun immediately disappeared. Sambat shepherded us towards the street, where we found Sarun waiting with a taxi. He motioned us all to climb in and somehow we all squeezed in. Sarun sat in front with Somaly on his knee, while Sambat, Da, Panita and I squashed into the back seat. Somaly and Panita were both hungry and thirsty and they immediately began to ask for something to fill their empty stomachs. The Khmer language made the driver look up and Sarun, noticing his curiosity, explained that we came from the Thai province of Surin, where 90% of the Thai people speak Khmer in their home villages. He seemed satisfied and drove on.

I had been absorbed in dealing with the children's questions but now, as the taxi swerved from side to side, I looked up. I was not prepared for what I saw. There were cars everywhere and they seemed to be going in all different directions. There was a cacophony of sound as each driver felt the necessity to hold his hand down on the horn. The driver of our taxi drove with one hand on the wheel and seemed very nonchalant about the cars whizzing past on each side. At one stage we stopped at a set of traffic lights. As we waited, motor-bikes sidled up through the gaps between the cars and waited with their engines revving as if they were at the starting line of some special race. As soon as the lights went green, they roared off leaving us clothed in a thick fog of exhaust fumes. It didn't seem to be long before we turned off the main road and went down a small side street. Right at the end, the taxi stopped and Sarun told us to get out. He paid the driver, who then turned around and went off to look for other passengers.

Sarun rang the bell on the side of the gate, and we looked through the bars to see who would come to open it. We saw Robert walking towards us, but he broke into a run when he realised who we were. We all greeted each other happily and Robert led us inside, all the time asking questions. "How on earth did you manage to get here?" "Who brought you?" He was very surprised that we had managed to get to Bangkok without any difficulty and Sarun began to explain about Jeremy's help and the journey.

It was only 12.30 p.m. but it felt like the end of the day as we had accomplished so much. We sat down to eat lunch and, at last, Somaly and Panita could eat and drink to their hearts' content. They were famished and the effects of the sleeping tablet had certainly worn off. They chattered away and never seemed to have enough answers to all their questions. They had gone to sleep on a straw mat in a refugee camp last night and now they were sitting down at a table eating a good meal on crockery instead of tin plates. There were certainly some changes in store for them in the next few weeks.

After lunch we all felt like going to sleep, but Robert bundled us into his pick-up truck and drove us off to the British Embassy. He parked outside and led us in through the front gate past a stern-looking Gurkha guard. We went up some stairs and into the Consular Section. Everything was ready and the Consul came out to welcome us with stacks of visa application forms that had to be filled in. Sitting down at a table, Robert filled them in for us and then we all had to sign. I was able to sign the forms for Somaly and Panita. As soon as those were done, they were whisked away, so that our identity documents could be prepared with the British entry visa stamped on them. Everything was happening so fast that my brain was in a whirl. The Consul came out again and shook hands with us. "Well, good luck to you all. I'm sure everything will be fine and I hope you have a good flight to England." Turning to Robert, he continued: "Here's a letter to the Immigration Division. If you have any problem, just give me a call. However, I think you'll find that they will do the process quite quickly." Robert thanked him and we were off again.

Weaving through the traffic, Robert explained that we had one more call to make that afternoon. We had to get to ICM to make sure that the flights were organised for Thursday night. Once again, everything was ready for us. The ICM officials were waiting. In fact, they appeared to be quite concerned. "Where have you been?" they asked Robert. "We had a telex from our Geneva office last week, saying that these four people should be on the flight Thursday night, but we haven't been able to track them down." Robert soothed their ruffled feathers and explained why it had been difficult to get us to Bangkok. They understood right away and bustled about making all the arrangements.

They took our identity documents so that they could make the necessary arrangements for the exit visa. This was necessary since we were 'illegal entrants'. Being refugees, we had crossed the border into Thailand without going through the formality of asking for a visa at a Thai Embassy first! That, naturally, would have been impossible, but it did mean that there were certain procedures to be gone through before we could leave the country. Robert explained that this meant we would have to present ourselves to the Immigration Division the next day. In effect, we would be surrendering ourselves to go through the formal procedure of being charged as illegal entrants.

Leaving the ICM office, which was situated on Patpong Road, the red-light area of Bangkok, Robert drove us to the big central department store on Ploenchitr Road. He parked the car in the underground car park. Somaly's and Panita's eyes were wide with wonder as we went up the stairs into the store. This was a totally mind-boggling experience for the girls. They ran from counter to counter gazing at all the items for sale. Robert took us round several different sections of the store and made sure that we had enough clothes and shoes for our journey to England. Somaly and Panita looked very smart in their new clothes and they had a look of disbelief on their faces as if to say, 'Pinch me and I'll wake up.' We went back to the house, ate supper and then stayed up late talking about all the things that had taken place that day.

Even so, we were up early the next morning and Robert took us to the Immigration Division. Sarun and Sambat had to wait outside to ensure that the police did not question them about their presence in Bangkok. Sambat decided that he would go off and see Bangkok on his own since he could do no more to help. Before he left he arranged to meet Robert back at the house that evening. We trooped into the building with some trepidation, although Robert's presence gave me some reassurance. The Illegal Entry Section was on the third floor. There were not many civilians there, just lots of police. We were taken to meet the section chief, who was a police major. He was very pleasant and I began to relax. After meeting him, we were taken from office to office to fill in a number of forms. Robert stayed with us and I was glad that he did, for we were closely questioned about our entry into Thailand and about how we travelled from the border to Bangkok.

The questioning was done in English, since none of the Thai police spoke Khmer and I didn't speak Thai. At one point, the policeman asked me: "Did you pay any money to come to Bangkok?" I thought back to our journey and remembered that Sarun had purchased the train tickets for 32 Baht, so I replied very simply, "Yes, 32 Baht." There was an immediate look of interest on the policeman's face. He looked up from his desk and started to call all the other policemen over. He spoke to them in Thai and I wondered what all the commotion was about. The policemen were gathered around me in a tight circle and I began to be afraid. Had I said something wrong? What were they saying to each other? My heart gave a jump as Robert's English voice suddenly cut into the Thai chatter. "She misunderstood your question."

The policemen quietened down and turned to Robert: "What do you mean?" one of them asked.

"She thought you were asking how much money she paid for her train ticket. It cost her 32 Baht."

As Robert's words sank in, the police roared with laughter and dispersed back to their own desks. I looked at Robert in bewilderment. A few minutes later, while the policeman was away getting some more forms, Robert told me that the policeman was asking if I had bribed any police to let us through a checkpoint. When I had said "Yes", they became all excited because they thought they had uncovered some corruption. I'll have to watch my words carefully, I thought to myself. I translated everything to

Da and the children so that they would not be afraid at
what was going on. We all relaxed and from then on, it
went quite smoothly.

Shortly before noon, the policeman stood up and said:
"That's all for this morning. Go away and get some lunch
and then be back here at 1 p.m. We'll take you to the court
for the hearing." It all seemed so easy. If we were illegal
entrants, why where they letting us out before everything
was settled? Robert couldn't explain it and I wasn't about
to ask the policeman. We left quickly and went to a small
restaurant just down the street. Sarun came with us and we
ate rice and pork for lunch. There were many people there
and we were treated to a number of stares as the Thai
people saw a bearded foreigner sitting with a group of
Asians. We had barely swallowed our last mouthfuls of rice
before Robert, glancing at his watch, stood up and said:
"OK, it's time to get back to the Immigration building.
We have a date with a judge to keep."

Arriving back at Immigration, we found two officials
waiting to escort us to the Court, which was on the other
side of the city. There was also a group of several other
foreigners who had overstayed their visas and who now
had to go to the Court to pay a fine. The officials conversed
with each other in Thai as they looked at us all. Sarun
moved closer to Robert and said: "They have a problem
because there are too many people to fit into their vehicle."
Robert seized the opportunity: "Please tell them that I have
a pick-up truck and would be glad to help them take
everyone to the Court." Sarun introduced himself to the
two officials as being Robert's assistant and then translated
Robert's offer into Thai. There were smiles all round at
this solution to their problem. The other group of
foreigners went with the officials and we all climbed into
Robert's truck. Robert drove out into the street following
the Immigration vehicle.

It was the lunch-time rush hour and it took us quite a

while to reach the other side of the city. By the time we got there, we were all very hot and sticky. Robert hunted round for a place to park and eventually squeezed his car into a small space not too far from the Court building. Robert and Sarun led the way, glancing round occasionally to make sure that we had not disappeared. One of the officials was waiting for us on the steps of the Court house. The other man was inside with the group of foreigners. We stood in the entrance hallway while waiting for our turn to go before the judge. Robert stood close to us and tried to cheer us up. We were feeling very apprehensive about it all and wondered if everything would really turn out well. Perhaps the judge would sentence us to several years in prison for entering Thailand illegally. Robert occasionally picked Panita up and carried her around the hallway.

We could see Sarun standing off to one side in deep conversation with some of the Court officials. After a while he came over to where we were standing. "I've just been talking to the officials," he began, "and I just happened to mention that I also spoke Khmer as well as Thai. They've asked me if I would act as the official Court interpreter since they don't have anyone who can speak Khmer to explain the proceedings to you. They all think I'm Thai because I speak it so well."

Robert gazed at Sarun in disbelief. Then he began to laugh. Both he and Sarun found it highly amusing that Sarun, a refugee, should act as the official interpreter.

At long last, we were all summoned to go before the judge. The Court had been set up at the end of a corridor, and I could only assume that they were short of rooms. Robert was asked to stand at one side while Da, Somaly, Panita and I were taken before the bench. Sarun stood next to one of the Court officials. We stared at the empty chair in front of us and wondered what the next move would be. A door opened and an older Thai man walked out. He was dressed in a black gown and had a most severe expression on his face. Here comes our jail sentence, I thought. The court official stepped forward and read quickly from some documents. Then he motioned to Sarun, who also stepped forward and the official continued speaking. He was obviously introducing the 'official' interpreter.

The judge glanced at us and said a few words in Thai. Sarun interpreted, "You have committed an illegal act by crossing the border into Thailand without first seeking a visa. According to the law, you must therefore pay a fine. There is no fine for the children, but the two adults must pay 1,400 Baht each." This was equivalent to about £35 each and I glanced at Robert hoping that he had enough money. Certainly neither Da nor I had more than about 50 Baht each. The judge stood up and walked out through the door. I looked from Da to Sarun and then to Robert. Was that it? Robert smiled and shrugged his shoulders. Sarun was speaking again to the official who was pointing to a glass window at the other end of the corridor. He gathered us together and Sarun spoke to Robert. "We just have to pay the fine and then we are free to go back to Immigration to finalise the paperwork." Robert walked off to pay the fines, while Sarun led us back to the car and then we were off once more.

Back at Immigration, we found an ICM man waiting. He had all our papers with him – identity documents, British visas, plane tickets and, most important of all, Thai exit visas. There were a number of forms which still had to be completed and then these had to be signed by several different police officers. However, finally, at 4.45 p.m., we were free to go. The ICM man spoke to Robert: "The plane tomorrow night doesn't leave until 10.30 p.m., but they must be at the airport by 6.30 p.m. so that we have time to process all the papers through Passport Control. Also, there are still some more forms to be signed at ICM and I think they will have to go for an X-ray and a medical check tomorrow." Robert promised to take care of all those things and we all piled into the car once more.

At the house that evening, I could hardly believe it. The plan was working. But, surely something would go wrong. I told myself off for my lack of faith. God was surely powerful enough to deal with all these little things, if he could keep us all alive through the terrible Khmer Rouge years. I relaxed and began to thank God for His faithfulness. Despite all my fears and concerns, He had brought me through many dangers and difficulties and it was silly of me not to place my full trust in Him.

Thursday, May 24th, 1979, dawned bright and clear. My last day in Thailand, I thought with a certain sense of satisfaction at the prospect of a new life in England. The day passed quickly in a kaleidoscope of events. There was a quick visit to Immigration again – this time to the medical section, where we had to have smallpox and cholera injections. Somaly and Panita didn't look too happy when they saw the needle and I must say that I didn't relish the thought of the needle in my arm either. Robert stepped to the front of the line and rolled up his sleeve. He asked me to translate to the girls that it really didn't hurt and he would have his injections first just to prove it. They watched Robert's face as the needle plunged in, but he kept on smiling. Satisfied, they held out their arms and the nurse gave the injections.

From Immigration, we drove to the Bangkok General Hospital for our medical exam. Out of all the tests that we were given, the eye test stands out in my memory. Somaly was shown a board hanging on a wall and was asked to read the numbers, which were written in both Thai and English. Somaly had been learning how to count in both Thai and English in the camp, and now she became totally confused as she read off the numbers. She said one word in Thai and another in English. It made the doctor and nurses roar with laughter.

Back at the house in the afternoon, Da and I packed and

repacked our few belongings. We ate an early supper and left the house at 5.30 p.m. Roy Clarke, one of Robert's friends, was going to England on the same plane as us and he would take care of us when we arrived in England. The large concrete buildings of the airport loomed up and we climbed out of the car. Robert asked Sarun and Sambat to take us into the check-in area, while he went off to park the car. Inside, we were greeted by the ICM man, who took our papers and went away to process everything. Robert joined us and we went to the check-in counter with our bags. It didn't take long to check them in and then there was nothing more to do except wait.

The waiting seemed endless. Panita was sad because she realised that she would have to say good-bye to Bhou Bear. Sarun and Da sat together and talked quietly. There was a growing bond between them both and they were sad at the forthcoming separation. I sat back in the chair as Robert took some pictures of us all and my mind retraced the events of the past few days. So much had happened and there was so much to thank God for. Not only had He brought us safely out of Cambodia, but He had also saved my arm when I was sick with anthrax and now He was bringing us out of Thailand.

A voice in Thai and then in English boomed out over the airport loudspeakers. They were announcing the departure of our flight to London – London – I thrilled to the sound of the name. We gathered up our bags. One by one we all put our hands together in front of our faces in the Khmer way to say good-bye. Then Robert picked up both the children to give them a hug and to say good-bye. Panita began to cry. She wanted Bhou Bear to come with us. She had grown very fond of him over the previous two months and now it was hard to say good-bye. "Tell her that I'll be in England at the end of next month and that I'll expect her to be able to speak English by then," Robert said, trying to distract her thoughts and asking me to interpret.

I told Panita and she cheered up a little. Then it was time to move forward to the Passport Control Section. I presented all of our papers and the officer quickly looked at them before stamping them and handing them back to me.

We moved past the barrier and turned to wave good-bye to the three men. The final part of our journey to Bangkok would have been impossible without them.

The ICM man appeared in front of us and led us through the various security checks. Having missed Bhou Bear tremendously, Panita had cried herself to sleep and Roy carried her on to the airport bus and then up the steps into the plane. We were shown to our seats and sank down. I showed Da and the girls how to put on their seat belts and we settled back for the take-off. We did not have long to wait and then we were airborne. My memory is hazy about that flight, but I sensed that we were drawing closer to freedom and a new life.

My memory is absolutely clear about our arrival in England. As we approached Heathrow airport, I looked down first at the green fields and then at the rows of houses and larger buildings that made up London. We landed safely and the plane taxied to a halt. As we walked off the plane and into the Arrivals Building, a few men with cameras rushed up and began taking photographs. I looked behind me to see who was the subject of the pictures, but everyone else seemed to be filing past the photographers without looking at them. It was only when someone said, "Smile, please," that I realised *we* were the ones being photographed! Several newspapers knew of our story through the Thames Television programme and had heard of our arrival. They wanted to be the first to print our pictures in their papers.

As we all walked out of the airport terminal, the sense of freedom became very real to me. I felt like doing a little dance and shouting, "We're free!"

13 Paradise

Christian Outreach, a British organisation that worked among refugees, took care of us in England. We were allowed to stay in their 'half-way' house in Godalming, which welcomed several refugees as they were resettled there. We were warmly welcomed by Robert's parents, Marion and Pat Ashe, who were both extremely kind and helpful. Pat was then Chairman of Christian Outreach. I gradually came to know many people in Godalming, both Christians and non-Christians, and they were without exception willing to go out of their way to help. When I think back to all the things that were done for me and given to me, I want to cry with gratitude.

Although I had travelled to different countries before the fall of Phnom Penh, I had not visited the west, and England was my first experience. I was more fortunate than many other refugees who arrived in England, since I already spoke English fairly well. It enabled me to understand what was going on and to find my way around without too much difficulty. After my years of starvation, I liked best the pleasure of walking up and down the aisles of the local supermarket and seeing the range of food available. Whatever I stinted on, it was never food. When I had been under the Khmer Rouge, I had promised myself that, if I ever escaped from that situation, I would never again allow myself or my children to go hungry.

England, with its freedom and friendliness, was easy to fall in love with after the forced labour that I had experienced in Cambodia, and I gradually learned to relax. Although I quickly recovered an outward appearance of health, I was not the same as before. My memory, in particular, had suffered, and I must often have appeared absent-minded and scatter-brained in the eyes of others. However, for Somaly and Panita it was a different matter and they soon began to benefit from attendance at St Hilary's, a private school not far from where we lived, thanks to an anonymous benefactor who paid for the school fees. The personal attention that they received at the school enabled them to learn English very fast. They quickly made friends with the other children and settled into the English way of life. I found that I began to have difficulty in getting them to remember their Khmer language!

Robert came to see us during his visit to England at the end of June 1979. Somaly and Panita were delighted to see him. In my own way, I was too. I had grown to like and respect this bearded man who had at first scared me. He had helped to save my family from being sent back to Cambodia and had been intimately involved in every aspect of the plan to get us to freedom. I was extremely grateful to him.

During the second half of 1979, the terrible suffering that Cambodia had experienced in the previous four years gradually became known to the rest of the world. Horrific pictures of death and starvation were revealed on British television and the image of a hell on earth burst into people's living rooms. The *Blue Peter* children's television programme began a campaign to raise funds for relief work to be carried out among those who had survived the Khmer Rouge régime. At one point, Somaly, Panita and I were asked to appear on the programme. It was an exciting time and we enjoyed going into the television studio. I explained a little of our story and thanked all the British people on behalf of the Cambodians for all the help that was being sent to my country. The response from the British people was phenomenal and my heart went out to them for their generosity.

At the Christian Outreach house I was asked to become the housekeeper to take care of the house and all the other refugees who passed through. It was a job that I enjoyed and was one way in which I could express my thanks to Christian Outreach. In addition, I also went to sewing classes and was able to become quite good at making clothes or sewing up curtains and chair covers. Several of my friends came to ask me to help them in some of their sewing projects.

Through the help of some friends, I was able to establish contact with my mother and other brother and sisters who were still in Cambodia. They had returned to Phnom Penh and found that our old house had been destroyed by fire either by the Khmer Rouge or by the Vietnamese. However, they were able to find a small empty house somewhere in the city and to set up home there. Life was difficult for my mother as, during the years under the Khmer Rouge, she had become blind and was now constantly dependent on other people to be her eyes. Away from the terror of the Khmer Rouge, my brother and sisters found jobs with the new Vietnamese-backed régime in an effort to help rebuild Cambodia from the horrors of the previous ten years. The occasional letters that I received from my family contained no news of my husband, Virak Phong. I knew that, if he was alive, either he would somehow have made contact with them, or he would have made an attempt to escape across the border into Thailand. My enquiries with the International Red Cross brought no results, and I gradually came to accept that he must be dead.

News came from Cambodia that my younger brother, Rathana, was still alive. I gazed at the letter in almost disbelief and my eyes blurred with tears. Rathana, who had walked out of my life in 1975 because of his intense desire to study, was alive. He had joined the exodus from Phnom Penh in April 1975 and had also managed to survive. After the Vietnamese invasion at the end of 1978, he had returned to Phnom Penh and had sought out my mother, who was overjoyed to have him near her again.

From Thailand we had many letters from Sarun. They kept us informed of the situation there, but most of his letters were to Da. Soon after we arrived in England, he was able to go and resettle in the United States. In less than a year, he came over to England and married Da in Godalming. Both of them were very happy and went back to America to begin their lives together there.

When I had been in the refugee camp in Thailand, my first preference had been to go to America or to France. I had not really considered England, as I had heard that the English people were very reserved and not all that friendly. However, after living in England for several months, I found that my expectations did not conform to reality. I found that, in general, English people were kind, helpful, modest and warm-hearted. Only twice during my first couple of years there did I come across two people who told me off for choosing England as my country of asylum and said that I should go back to the place from where I had come. At the time, the two incidents upset me but I was able to understand their feeling that England should only be for the English. I only wished that they could also understand that, if I had the choice and if my country were at peace again, I would like nothing better than to return to my homeland and my family. Since the majority of people whom I met were so good to me, it was easy for me to settle down and to be thankful that I had been allowed to resettle in England. By and large, I was astonished at the welcome shown to me.

While my life in England was happy, there was still a gap in my life because my husband was almost certainly dead. I had made many friends who were a constant support to me and I will be forever grateful to them. They relieved my loneliness, but they could not replace it.

Robert began to write letters to me from Thailand. He wrote about his work and also enquired about the children. He wanted to know how they were doing in school, how their English was progressing and so on. Little by little, his letters began to take on a more personal note. To begin with, I was not sure of what he was trying to say and yet I found myself responding in a similar way. The friendship between us grew and strengthened as we continued to exchange letters after our arrival in England. In fact, it became a long-distance courtship which filled the loneliness in my heart. Although he was busy with his work, he often wrote an average of two or three times a week and my heart would thrill every time I heard the post coming through the letter-box each morning. Life began to take on a new meaning.

His love for the Khmer people was obvious and he continued to work tirelessly on their behalf. During the first half of 1980 he worked along the Thai-Cambodian border and was often exposed to the dangers of war during the fighting that constantly took place there. He established what came to be known as the 'human land-bridge' at a camp called Nong Chan. There, working with the International Committee for the Red Cross, he set up a food distribution system where he was able to distribute food, rice seed and agricultural tools to 20,000 people a day. The items were carried into Cambodia on people's backs, on bicycles and on ox-carts, and helped to reduce the pressure of refugees coming to the border in search of food during 1980, as well as helping to rehabilitate agriculture in western Cambodia.

In June 1980, in recognition of his contribution to the welfare of Cambodian refugees in Thailand, he was made an MBE (Member of the Order of the British Empire) by the Queen. The news of this award had barely reached us when we heard that, in late June 1980, he had been captured by Vietnamese troops while working to evacuate wounded people from the middle of a combat zone. I wondered what had happened to him. Along with his parents, Pat and Marion Ashe, and many other people around the world, I prayed for his deliverance. I could not bear the thought of losing someone else whom I had grown to love. I need not have worried. Our Father has infinite power and He was more than able to protect Robert. Three days after his capture, the Vietnamese released him, none the worse for his experience.

In 1981 I received a surprise letter from an old friend of mine, Samnang, who had escaped to Thailand in 1980 and had then been accepted for resettlement in the United States shortly afterwards. She had heard from a mutual friend that I was still alive in England. We had been very close friends in Phnom Penh before the war and had gone to teacher training college together. I had lost touch with her shortly before the fall of Phnom Penh in April 1975 and had no idea what had happened to her. Now she was writing to me from America. She had an amazing story to tell, but she also had news for me of Virak Phong, which she had heard from another mutual friend in Phnom Penh in late 1979.

In early 1976 Virak Phong had flown back to Phnom Penh via Peking along with several hundred other Khmer intellectuals. All along the way they were told of the wonderful advances that the communists had made in the new 'Kampuchea'. They were told of how they would be able to use their skills to help in the enormous task of rebuilding their country. As they left the plane at Pochentong Airport in Phnom Penh, they were all seized, their belongings confiscated and then they were thrown into prison for being tainted with the capitalism of the west. It was an unfair accusation (as all forms of communism are unfair) since the Khmer Rouge leaders themselves had studied at the Sorbonne University, Paris, in the 1950s and 1960s. Some of the returnees were sent away from Phnom Penh to work as forced labour in opening up new forested areas for agriculture. However, many – including Virak Phong – were left to languish in prison, often undergoing torture to force them to confess to their 'crimes' against the Angkar. Virak Phong fell very ill and his natural resistance to diseases was gradually eroded. He eventually died in prison towards the end of 1976.

Samnang went to the prison in Phnom Penh where Virak Phong had been held by the Khmer Rouge. The Vietnamese had cleaned the place up after capturing the city early in 1979. In the prison they found the meticulous records of the people who had been imprisoned there. There were names and other details and the dates when people had died. The Vietnamese had taken the lists of those who had died and had pasted them on the walls of the prison for relatives who came in search of their loved ones. There on the lists Samnang found the name of Virak Phong. Date of death – 1976.

It was not much of an epitaph for the man whom I had loved and who was the father of my two children. I read the news contained in Samnang's letter and, although my mind had long ago accepted the fact of his death, I still felt a terrible sense of loss. Somaly and Panita, also, had come to realise that they would never see their father again. Panita was only a year old when she had last seen him and she could not remember him. However, the news of his death touched Somaly more, for she was five when he had boarded the plane for Paris in 1974. She remembered him well and loved him dearly. Time is a great healer and, although none of us will ever forget him, the emotional scars are now healed and we can look to the future, as we know that he would have wanted us to do.

Later in 1981 I was offered a job in a Christian bookshop called the 'Good News Centre', then run by South-east Asian Outreach. The shop was in Swindon and entailed a move from Godalming. I had made many friends in

Godalming and was reluctant to leave them. However, the possibility of a job there encouraged me to consider it. Somaly had just been accepted for Wadhurst College, a boarding school in Sussex. This was a Christian school with a good reputation. Although the fees were much more than I could possibly afford, even if I had a job, the Lord provided wonderfully. The school gave her a bursary which covered more than half the costs and an anonymous donor provided the rest. This meant that Panita would have to change schools. She was getting on so well at St Hilary's that it was less than the best solution. I made my decision to move and, when the moving-day dawned, several friends came to help me pack and to drive me to Swindon. We settled in the home of a family who were away on a two-year Bible-training course.

Since arriving in England, I had begun to attend church in Godalming and then afterwards in Swindon. My contacts with other Christians were of great importance to me not only in strengthening my faith, but also in helping me adjust to a new life. Some of my non-Christian friends told me that I didn't need to call myself a Christian – all I needed was to do good. They considered Christians to be hypocritical and, in some cases, I suppose they were right, since Christians are also human and make mistakes like everyone else. However, because of my own experience concerning the power of God's love, my faith was too strong to be affected by what people said to me. My belief in God was an important factor in making me a different person than I might otherwise have been.

In April 1982 Robert returned to England on one of his infrequent visits. He was now working for a French organisation and had a few weeks' holiday. On April 14th he visited us in Swindon. While we were sitting talking, he got down on one knee and pulled a little box from his pocket. Opening it, he took out a ring which glowed with a bright blue Cambodian sapphire. "Will you marry me?"

he asked. I gasped with joy and flung my arms around his neck. It was several moments later when he reminded me that I had not given him an answer in the midst of my excitement. "Yes," I replied, "a million times, yes!"

Although we were almost certain that Somaly and Panita would be happy to have Robert as their new father, we wanted to be sure that they also would be happy about our plans to marry. A few days later, Robert was back again in Swindon and we called Somaly and Panita together. We told them of our plans and asked them what they thought. Their rather casual, "I don't mind," masked a happiness which soon began to reveal itself in their smiling faces.

The next couple of weeks, which was all that Robert had left in England before he had to return to his work in Thailand, rushed by. There were so many plans to be made. The first decision that Robert made was that he would give up his work in Thailand. After seven years there, he felt that he had done all that he could for now. Besides, we both felt the need to get to know each other as part of a family and this would not have been possible if Robert and I were in Thailand while Somaly and Panita were at school in England.

The next important decision was when and where we would have the wedding. As soon as Robert had asked me to marry him, I called Patsy Merryweather, who had been a wonderful friend to me, to tell her the good news. Then her husband, Reggie, called to say that he would be delighted to act as a surrogate father to me and to arrange the wedding. It was an answer to prayer. Patsy and Reggie lived in a small hamlet called Paradise in the village of Painswick in Gloucestershire. The wedding would be in the parish church and the reception would be in Paradise. I already felt that I was in paradise, so it was most appropriate. We fixed the date for August 7th and Robert said that he would tie up his work and hand over to a successor by the beginning of July.

August 7th dawned bright and clear. The service was due to start at midday but preparations started long before that. Somaly and Panita were my bridesmaids and both of them looked lovely. Patsy drove them off to the church to wait at the porch while Reggie and I waited to be the customary few minutes late. There were crowds of well-wishers outside the church and even some journalists and television cameras, which made me nervous. The day before the wedding, Robert and I had been interviewed by two television crews outside the church, one after the other. They were there again on the wedding day and the sight of them increased my nervousness. As we reached the porch, the organ music started up and we began the procession inside. There, at the front of the church, was Robert together with his best man, Harvey Williams. Robert smiled at me and I felt more at ease. Robert's father, Pat, conducted the service and Roy Clarke, who had escorted us on the plane from Thailand to England, gave the sermon. While we were in the church office signing all the forms, the little choir sang the lovely song, "When I needed a neighbour, were you there?" The refrain, "And the creed and colour and the name won't matter," signified to me the complete acceptance that Robert, his family and friends had for me, a stranger from a country far away.

After the service was over, there were many pictures to be taken before Robert and I were driven off to the reception in Paradise. Patsy and Reggie had organised the reception as if I was a royal bride. There was a marquee in their garden and masses of food. In his speech, Reggie spoke of me as if I was one of his own daughters, which made me feel so much at home and a part of the family. As Robert and I walked to the car after the reception to drive away for our honeymoon on the Welsh border, Panita came running up and gave him a big hug. I was part of a family that was whole once more and that completed my happiness.

Epilogue

Following our short honeymoon in Wales, Robert and I collected Somaly and Panita, who had stayed with friends after the wedding, and we went off to France for a holiday. By the end of August we were back in Swindon, and it was time to get the girls ready to go back to school. Panita was starting her first term at Wadhurst College and I was going to miss her not being in the house all the time. It was also time for Robert to begin the task of seriously looking for a new job. He had already sent off several letters and now he also began to scan the papers. The next several months were spent in writing more letters and travelling to interviews. Robert even left for 10 days to go to California to be interviewed for a position with World Vision, an international relief agency. He had initially hoped to find a job in England so that we could begin to establish a stable family base. However, after six months, we began to wonder if the Lord was directing us overseas again, and so Robert wrote to a number of overseas agencies. Within a month, he had been accepted for a position in Thailand with Food for the Hungry International, a relief and development organisation which was based in Geneva. We made preparations for a move once more.

Now that Robert had a secure job, we felt that the time had come to plan for an addition to our family. We were overjoyed to discover in September that I was pregnant. I had just found a job for myself in Bangkok, with another relief agency, Operation Handicap International, and I was their administrative assistant. I suffered a little from morning sickness, but was able to continue working until March 1984. I enjoyed my work which involved dealing with administration and accounts, translating from French to English and writing reports. I was sad when the time came finally to give it up due to the imminent birth of my child.

In February 1984, Robert was called away to Bolivia to deal with an administrative crisis that had arisen there. He was away for five weeks, but got back in plenty of time for the birth of the baby. He came with me into both the labour room and the delivery room and gave me considerable comfort and support. As the baby was born, he came round to me and said: "Congratulations. You've produced our first son and the first grandson in both of our families."

Before our son was born we had all discussed together what we would call him. Robert preferred the name Peter, whereas I had always thought of him as Richard. Somaly had her heart set on calling him Mark and Panita wanted him to be Luke. In the end, we wrote the four names on four separate pieces of paper and put them in a hat. Robert mixed them up and then pulled the first piece out. It read, 'Peter'.

So Peter it was, and he was a joy to us in spite of the sleepless nights! Both Somaly and Panita fell in love with him and helped to take loving care of him. The date of his birth was April 17th, 1984, the ninth anniversary of the fall of Phnom Penh – an easy date to remember and a reminder of God's goodness to me since that awful day, nine years earlier, when my country was plunged into four years of terrible suffering.